A God Torn to Pieces

Studies in Violence, Mimesis, and Culture

SERIES EDITOR

William A. Johnsen

The Studies in Violence, Mimesis, and Culture Series examines issues related to the nexus of violence and religion in the genesis and maintenance of culture. It furthers the agenda of the Colloquium on Violence and Religion, an international association that draws inspiration from René Girard's mimetic hypothesis on the relationship between violence and religion, elaborated in a stunning series of books he has written over the last forty years. Readers interested in this area of research can also look to the association's journal, *Contagion: Journal of Violence, Mimesis, and Culture.*

A God Torn to Pieces

The Nietzsche Case

Giuseppe Fornari

Translation by Keith Buck
in collaboration with the author

Michigan State University Press · *East Lansing*

♾ The paper used in this publication meets the minimum requirements of ANSI/NISO Z39.48-1992 (R 1997) (Permanence of Paper).

 Michigan State University Press
East Lansing, Michigan 48823-5245

Printed and bound in the United States of America.

19 18 17 16 15 14 13   1 2 3 4 5 6 7 8 9 10

LIBRARY OF CONGRESS CATALOGING-IN-PUBLICATION DATA
Fornari, Giuseppe, 1956–
A God torn to pieces : the Nietzsche case / Giuseppe Fornari.
pages cm. — (Studies in violence, mimesis, and culture series)
Includes bibliographical references and index.
ISBN 978-1-60917-392-0 (ebook) — ISBN 978-1-61186-101-3 (pbk. : alk. paper)
1. Nietzsche, Friedrich Wilhelm, 1844–1900—Religion. 2. Christianity—Philosophy.
I. Title.
B3318.C35F67 2013
193—dc23
2012049439

Book design by Charlie Sharp, Sharp Des!gns, Lansing, Michigan
Cover design by David Drummond, Salamander Design, www.salamanderhill.com
Cover sketch was drawn by Friedrich Nietzsche in his journal when he was around ten years old.

g green press INITIATIVE Michigan State University Press is a member of the Green Press Initiative and is committed to developing and encouraging ecologically responsible publishing practices. For more information about the Green Press Initiative and the use of recycled paper in book publishing, please visit *www.greenpressinitiative.org*.

Visit Michigan State University Press at *www.msupress.org*

Contents

A Strange Debt to Europe

... this time I shall come as victorious Dionysus, who will make this world a holiday ... Not that I have much time ... [...] I have been hanged on the cross, too ...

—Nietzsche to Cosima Wagner, January 3, 1889[1]

... e quindi uscimmo a riveder le stelle.
[... and thence we came forth to see again the stars.]

—Dante Alighieri, *Inferno*, XXXIV, 139[2]

I feel a certain emotion now at seeing this study on Nietzsche, written several years ago, finally published in the United States, while I am quite curious to discover how it will fare in a cultural context very different from the Italian intellectual environment in which I first became acquainted with his works, in the late seventies. However, my emotion has also a more direct connection. As a matter of fact, the initial impulse to write this essay came to me in America, on my summer visits to Stanford University in the nineties for study and discussion sessions with René Girard, certainly some of the most fruitful encounters in my life, both intellectually and spiritually.

So, it is fair to say that the genesis of this book, which I regard as not the least important of my works in spite of its brevity, is closely bound up with the United States.

A God Torn to Pieces: The Nietzsche Case is the final result of an initial project, conceived around 1997 and 1998, to publish a collection of Girard's essays on Nietzsche, both in English and Italian, with a general introduction of mine to set out the particular problems raised by Nietzsche's philosophy and the far-reaching consequences of Girard's interpretation. For me this marked the point of deepest interaction and dialogue with Girard, and my work soon outgrew the bounds of a simple introduction. In view of its expansion and the relevance of the points I was exploring there, Girard generously suggested that we should co-author a work on Nietzsche for publication in English and Italian. This resulted in *Il caso Nietzsche*, which appeared in Italian in 2002,[3] while the English edition met several obstacles: the first was ideological prejudice from some American university publishers to whom I had submitted the project[4]; the second and more objective obstacle was the fact that most of Girard's essays on Nietzsche had already been published and re-published in America, as in the important anthology edited by James G. Williams, *The Girard Reader*.[5] Anyway, in order to make clear how I came to the present form of publication I should explain the path of research I followed in the late nineties.

To a degree that I had not expected, I discovered that the mimetico-sacrificial interpretation of Nietzsche interacted profoundly with my own grounding in philosophy, in which he had been a major influence. As I looked at Nietzsche through the mimetic lens, Girard's insights seemed to reveal their full interpretative power, not only for Nietzsche's writings but also for the striking evidence concerning his mental illness and final madness. Indeed, I found this so impressive that I decided to emphasize this aspect from the outset while analyzing his ideas (an act of sacrilege for any devotee of Nietzsche[6]). Girard's general thesis was significantly confirmed, and further proof given of his ability to grasp the essential both in texts and in human experience, but the subject itself and my approach to it involved something more than the demonstration of mimetic theory that I had had in mind in a period of my intellectual life still characterized to some extent by 'Girardian orthodoxy.' This is the main reason why I have now decided to let my research stand alone. In this way the accent falls on the independent line that I actually began to trace out in the nineties, following from my interaction with Girard's interpretation of Nietzsche.

We already partly differed in regard to method. It was not out of simple curiosity that I felt the need to start from the clinical reports of Nietzsche's madness, but because I aimed to glean relevant information from the very doubles crisis which drove him out of his mind. What struck me most strongly was the individual tragedy of this lonely man, for which I could feel nothing but sympathy, within the difficult situation of nineteenth century Europe, confronted by new dramatic collective experiences, and rightly defined in a book devoted to its decline in the following century as "a melting-pot brimful with creativity, discoveries, poetry, genius, and compressed violence."[7] We need to seriously consider this wider historical framework if we are to grasp the real meaning of 'the case of Nietzsche.' At that time the advanced echelons of European culture were discovering the violence lying at the root of human society; this increasing awareness has to be seen ultimately as closely linked to the upheavals produced by the many 'revolutions' deeply affecting European society over the centuries: the discovery of the New World, the breaking-up of medieval Christianity with the Reformation, the scientific and industrial revolutions, the French revolution, and finally the rise of nationalism and colonial imperialism. While artists, philosophers, and scientists managed to explore these unprecedented changes cognitively, European society failed to come to terms with them practically and eventually ended in disaster, as the history of the twentieth century was to demonstrate so dreadfully. I came to identify more and more closely with this collective and individual drama and began to see its inner logic more clearly, a logic that we are bound to recognize now. Here, too, I differ from Girard in part, but more as a question of content.

The cause of knowledge was well served by European culture around the turn of the twentieth century, with some amazing achievements in anthropology, culminating in Freud's *Totem and Taboo* in 1912–1913 (on the eve of the First World War), the groundbreaking systematic attempt to explain the origin of human culture from a collective murder. The genius of Freud consisted mainly in detecting ideas circulating in the German-speaking world and Europe. Freud's theory might never have reached formulation if Nietzsche's madman had not previously announced the collective murder of God, and in his turn Nietzsche was indebted to Wagner's extensive exploration of German mythology. And there were further impressive developments, more especially in the freer realm of imaginative literature, rather than in the stricter environment of philosophy and science. So, at this point, I thought to include some textual analyses of works by Gabriele D'Annunzio and Thomas Mann. Today I would certainly include Georges Bataille as well, who more than any other writer in the twentieth century continued with Nietzsche's human and cultural venture. More daring even than Nietzsche in his explorations, and more virile in his assumptions about erotic desire, Bataille, for these very reasons, comes much closer to accepting Christ. It is against this historical and cultural background that we need to see Girard if we are to understand him and appreciate his real significance.

On the basis of these premisses, I also differ from Girard in my evaluation of Nietzsche's relationship to Christianity. It is thanks to Girard that we can now recognize the undeniable importance of Nietzsche in the history of Christian thought, even though Christian culture itself still seems far from granting such recognition. However, it is in assessing Nietzsche's philosophy and fate that my conclusions are more distinctly personal. In my opinion Nietzsche cannot really be held responsible for the use made of his ideas by the Nazi regime. Undoubtedly some of those ideas, especially towards the end of his life, were irresponsible and sinister, and Girard was quite right to shake Nietzsche's admirers and scholars out of their dogmatic slumber. Nevertheless, my thesis is that Nietzsche was to a great extent a kind of early-warning device, perceiving well in advance where Europe was heading. Anticipatory of this, a few years before, was the pre-Nietzschean accent of the ideas attributed to Raskolnikov in Dostoevsky's *Crime and Punishment*. No doubt Dostoevsky disapproved of Raskolnikov's attitude; Nietzsche, on the contrary, shared and developed it, though towards the end of his mentally-conscious life he expressed admiration for Dostoevsky's art. However, we should not forget that Nietzsche killed no old women in order to demonstrate his superior human status but instead destroyed himself. Rather than ideological, his role was prophetic of what was about to happen in Europe. A glance at history here will make clearer the general tendency in Europe, at that time the world's most populous, rich, and powerful continent. We need to go back to before the catastrophe of the First World War to the last period of political and economic revolution in Europe.

It was no accident that awareness of the coming crisis in Europe was greater, as I see it, in countries that felt themselves unfairly situated in the international balance of power before the First World War, while colonial expansion, above all of England and France, was providing Western culture with a huge amount of comparative data on cultures and cults of extra-European peoples. Germany emerged reeling from the effects of the Napoleonic wars but, having lost its universal role as seat of the Holy Roman Empire, was denied national status at the Congress of Vienna and later, after 1871, neither France nor England would accept its economic and military predominance in continental Europe; Dostoevsky's Russia (another universal empire, a third Rome, heir to Byzantium) was torn between emulation of Western Europe and its ambition to form the heart of a new pan-Slav Europe; the Austrian empire, to some extent the heir of the old Holy Roman Empire, became virtually dependent on the German Reich after 1866 and there was an increasing awareness among the Viennese intelligentsia that their world was coming to an end; and the newly-united state of Italy, unified in 1861 counter to its polycentric history unfolding under the influence of the universal spiritual *auctoritas* of the Church, remained fragile while it aspired to equal status with the other European powers. French culture, in its turn, proved to be more sensitive to the aspects explored by Nietzsche as long as it was interacting with the growing national rivalry with Germany. After the Pyrrhic victory of the First World War, France paid increasing attention to those aspects as it waited for the German giant to take its predictable revenge: Bataille and his *Acéphale* (the headless man, a Nietzschean symbol for the sacrificial victim) is a perfect example of this intellectual climate.[8] This is the historical and cultural landscape evoked by Girard's personal testimony in *Achever Clausewitz*,[9] though he makes no mention of Bataille or any explicit connection with Nietzsche.

On the contrary, I consider Nietzsche's part in this story as essential. The subject has still to be fully explored within a more general study of how European thought conceived the relationship between *Kultur*, the culture linked to tradition and a sacred foundation, and *Zivilisation*, the breaking-down of all cultural and sacred boundaries in the melting-pot of what we now call globalization.[10] The opposing tendencies in the European countries more deeply involved in this debate were either to defend *Kultur* against the threat of *Zivilisation* or to invent new revolutionary forms of the latter, understood as the progress of capitalism and democracy or as a working class socialist revolution. But as a matter of fact the two tendencies intermingled and influenced each other mimetically, showing not only that the problem of defending the various *Kulturen* was real but also that their effective restoration was simply impossible. The result of such a conflicting situation was a multiplying of ideologies and political movements that led to the Bolshevik Revolution in 1917 and to the subsequent violent reactions, in a word to the infernal scenario of totalitarianism. Globalization has clearly shown that concern over the end of traditional *Kulturen*, a process now going on throughout the world, was by no means misplaced, but that we cannot go back to any simplistic solution, defensive and/or destructive. We can only look bravely to the future, but, in order not to do this blindly, we need to understand what happened in Europe between the nineteenth and twentieth century. A proper interpretation of Nietzsche has much to teach us about this, and I will come back shortly to these historical considerations.

Something more needs to be said now about the cultural and religious background against which all the upheavals described took place and were defined. Girard holds that Christianity was the direct or indirect cause of these huge changes since it destroyed the sacrificial coverings of the archaic and ancient cultures, bringing the cultural world influenced by the Gospel message face to face with the hidden truth of its own violence. According to Girard, the Western world for the most part went against this religious heritage, and Nietzsche is a perfect example of this mistaken attitude. Yet, I think that this Nietzschean and European tendency substantially differed from sheer nostalgia for ancient sacrifice. Girard is not completely right because he is more right than he might suspect, in the sense that the phenomena he has helped us to recognize are more radical than he supposes. And "more radical" both in the destructive and possibly creative meaning of the word. This is my different way of considering human mimesis, based on powerful structures of collective mediation which are not to be confused with more individual desires and are capable of exploiting their very destructive potential in a surprisingly creative way, though often at high cost.[11] Our capacity to find new resources and strategies can only attain its fullest realization when put in jeopardy, with no recognizable way out: our most effective hope erupts from despair. Nietzsche illustrates this ambivalence, or rather double bind, in the most disturbing fashion.

My study shows that Nietzsche nurtured hatred not only against Christianity but specifically against Christ himself, defined as "the idiot on the cross."[12] At first glance 'the Nietzsche case' would appear to be an exemplary story of "empio punito" (the ungodly one punished): the philosopher arrogantly defying Christ and being destroyed by his own foolishness; and Girard's interpretation in substance endorses this view. But this is actually only one aspect of a more complex personal drama, in which the most intimate experience proves to be the existential workshop for deeper anthropological and religious understanding, as Christianity leads us to understand and Girard teaches. Nietzsche was a victim from early childhood, suffering greatly on account of the loss of his father and then growing up in a limited and limiting environment. He admired and loved Wagner as a second father but at the same time was the victim of psychosis, regarding the composer as his unattainable paternal model, as his greatest friend *and* enemy. While Wagner's overwhelming personality gave the impulse to Nietzsche's creativity, it fatally revealed his inability to regain his lost father. In the unstable mind of Wagner's admirer this double paternal loss became a psychotic and metaphysical drama. Beyond the fathers of this world there was the Heavenly One, hated and envied in the person of his beloved Son. In the exalting and exalted atmosphere of the Wagnerian circle, and of a Germany in search of its 'intellectual god' ever since the time of Goethe and Hölderlin, Nietzsche strove to make himself the victorious, ferocious son of God, in a word, Dionysus. However, this attempt was made so openly that its character was transformed and became deeply disturbing, something at once old and new, exciting and dreadful, something like a self-crucified Dionysus-Christ.

It is the newness of Nietzsche's attempt that marks the principle change in my interpretation and, although it is potentially present in this study, I would develop it much further today. Nietzsche consciously sought to bring about a new super-humanity that would be capable of sacrifice while it knew that sacrifice was murder. His assurance grew that humanity could not go back to the old Dionysian sacrifice.[13] The dilemma of choosing between Dionysus and Christ thus came to be a 'trilemma,' in which Dionysus was the past, Christ was the rejected alternative, and only the third, terribly consistent and most revealing choice remained. Nietzsche was never so right as when he was wrong. He was unwilling to give up the incredible power of divinization, on which he set his hopes for victory and a new life as the victorious son who succeeded in killing his father (his manifold fathers). Yet a real god has no need to demonstrate his godhood to himself or others. And so the fatal consequence of this insane but lucid strategy of self-divinization was the sacrifice of himself, in order to show once and for all that he was divine. As he said himself, in the aphorism on the death of God: "Mustn't we become gods?" The question reveals its real meaning if we extend it to include not only Europe, but all mankind.

In this sense Nietzsche partially prophesized (but—I repeat—was not really responsible for) the original sacrificial logic introduced by the two main totalitarian regimes, Stalinism and Nazism. This is confirmed by Hannah Arendt, whose analyses are even more telling as they are explicitly independent of any scapegoat theory, and therefore of sacrificial foundation.[14] The point is that totalitarianism in no way attempts to restore the archaic sacrificial foundation, as Girard simplistically assumes.[15] On the contrary, it tries to invent a new dynamic sacrificial order, consisting in dehumanizing its victims so that killing them no longer constitutes a murder, but is an act of cleansing or elementary justice. This is possible because the totalitarian movements do not confine themselves to conquering the State but empty it from within, exploiting its administrative and legal machinery and leaving real power in the hands of the Party and its prestigious leader. A new random and ever-changing divinization arises, casting its sinister light on the totalitarian leader and his followers, even though in the debased context of mass propaganda and industrial and military power, a far cry from the aristocratic super-humanity that Nietzsche was dreaming of. This suggests a further consideration that I want at least to mention.

It would be foolish for us to presume that we are safely beyond such dreadful scenarios thanks to the victory of the 'forces with God on their side' in the Second World War (though one of them was a major totalitarian regime) and above all thanks to the final victory of democracy and capitalism following the end of the Cold War. We only need to recall the double bind between *Kultur* and *Zivilisation*.[16] Indeed, capitalism, the leading force in globalization, has the concrete possibility of becoming the updated version of a more advanced and subtle totalitarianism, with its hidden centers of decision-making and control able to transform democracy into a theatrical spectacle and to create new frontiers for victimization simply by declaring, mainly through the media, that the new victims have no right to exist or simply do not exist. And among these victims I would include the sense itself of cultural transmission, and the historical and spiritual diversity of the world's cultures and languages, that we should consider an essential part of our human heritage, and not a troublesome memory of a past that we had best forget.

Going back now to my inquiry into Nietzsche's life and thought, that was able to stimulate such meaningful analyses concerning our world, its conclusion provides a proper framework for reflections that might otherwise easily become too bitter or too apocalyptic. Actually, the same creativity shown by Nietzsche and, in a more perverse way, by the destructive experiments of totalitarianism suggests that at the very center of cultural destruction (destruction arising from cultures and destroying them) could lie our only hope of avoiding it. For this reason, I do not agree with the too one-sided apocalyptic view presented in Girard's *Achever Clausewitz*. Christianity is much more than a message about the end of the world to be taken too literally, and the end of Nietzsche provides us with unexpected confirmation of this. I will explain this last affirmation by telling how I wrote the two conclusive chapters of my essay, the most challenging part of my Nietzschean adventure.

Due to the very complexity of the subject, the penultimate chapter of my inquiry, which deals with Nietzsche's desperate attempt to destroy both Christ and Christianity, turned out to be a real battlefield for me while I was finishing my essay. Besides the difficulty of dealing with the doubles in Nietzsche's mind that were about to explode into open madness, there was the heartbreaking spectacle of an individual fighting against his destiny, seeking a truth so long and stubbornly denied that when at last he came to it, the effort proved fatal. To a certain extent I had to re-live that hellish journey and wrestle with the spirit of Nietzsche himself, rather like Jacob wrestling with the angel. Possibly I won the struggle thanks to that most powerful ally, compassion (in the etymological sense of *cum-passio*, suffering together), that is, my sense of pity for my opponent. Like Dante when he journeyed through Hell, though I moved on a more scholarly and mundane plane, real relief came to me only on returning to the surface again, to the more human environment of purgatory where compassion is the sole token for our hope of eventually going to heaven, and is itself the only heaven that we can know on earth. I believe that the spirit of Nietzsche informed this strange adventure.

Having successfully concluded that difficult passage, I was able to go on to the final, and spiritually most important, chapter, where I argue that there was no other way for Nietzsche to attempt to reach the unattainable Father except through his desperate challenge. Hatred was his distorted way of realizing an impossible love. In this sense, the poems written by Nietzsche that are examined in the last chapter—above all "Ruhm und Ewigkeit" ["Glory and Eternity"], whose last three stanzas are one of the most beautiful mystic texts of all time—are a telling expression of his destiny, strongly hinting that madness may have been his way to win a strange, inconceivable salvation. In the end he was much closer to Christ than many who would claim to be Christians. That is the final thought that I would like to leave with the reader.

Could it not also be a hopeful indication for the troublesome history of Europe and the world today? Not in the sense that we should become mad (or discover that we already are mad, without excluding this possibility) in order to achieve salvation, but in the sense that there are hidden spiritual and cultural resources on which we could draw paying much more attention to the most perilous and vital core of our recent past.

This translation, made in close collaboration with me, largely conforms to the Italian text published in 2002, apart from some changes of historical details and several passages where I felt the need to give a more balanced and sympathetic evaluation of Nietzsche's thought and destiny. I have added also in the last chapter some short texts useful to further illustrate my thesis, above all the amazing Christological "message of madness" that at the moment of the first Italian edition was not yet accessible in the critical edition of Nietzsche's letters, and the outstanding testimony of Overbeck when he went to Turin to aid his friend in his madness. Many additional endnotes, in square brackets, refer to further developments in my study of Nietzsche, and in my works of later date, which I hope to publish in English in the near future. In spite of their position at the end of the volume, they should be considered as an essential part of the text. *A God Torn to Pieces* must therefore be considered a new revised and updated edition of my essay, even though not to the extent I would have wished.

Quotations from Nietzsche's works and letters are directly made from the German text in its critical edition (Colli-Montinari), given that its English translation at Stanford University Press (in the very place where I wrote the very first version of my essay) is a huge project still far from being accomplished, and also for the sake of stylistic uniformity. For practical reasons I usually quote the pocket edition of Nietzsche's works and letters (*editio minor*), and the more detailed hardcover edition (*editio maior*) only for the texts not available there. Only in one case, a letter written by Elisabeth to Franziska Nietzsche, I was unable to find the German original, as a part of the indirect correspondence still has to be published in a critical edition and is found in old publications that are not readily available. I quote the Italian Colli-Montinari edition in the critical apparatus where it is more complete than in the German edition (this edition is a major achievement of the interest aroused by Nietzsche in Italian culture and its comments should be seen as part of the original project). Other primary sources are translated from the German or Italian original for the same reasons of stylistic uniformity, while some non-Italian sources are quoted from the Italian version for the cases in which there is not a precise equivalent to the Italian edition.

For the cover of the book I have chosen a juvenile drawing by Nietzsche, more subtle and eloquent than the usual pictures of him with his long moustache and short-sighted or hysterical look.[17] It represents a warrior seen from behind, raising an invisible sword with his right hand, against an invisible enemy. As we cannot see his face, he is an unseen hero fighting against the Unseen, an impossible mediator who cannot mediate anything as he is unattainable beyond Nietzsche's desire, looking at the Unconceivable. He is already an impossible memory and the ghost of Nietzsche's future.

My thanks are due to all those who have made it possible to publish this book: to René Girard, above all, who first set me off on this intellectual and personal adventure; to Peter Thiel whose generosity has made this translation possible, and to all the people at Imitatio, starting with the former president Bob Hamerton-Kelly and the current president Lindy Fishburne; to Jean-Pierre Dupuy, Research Committee Chair and Advisory Board member, to whom I am especially grateful for his personal interest; to Bill Johnsen for his constant encouragement to have my work published in English, and so bring discussion of these topics, vitally related both to our past and future, to a far wider audience.

CHAPTER 1

The Hunt for the Whale

The drama's done. Why then here does anyone step forth?—Because one did survive the wreck.

—Ishmael in *Moby Dick*[1]

The figure of Nietzsche is of fundamental importance for a better understanding of Christianity and its uniqueness; this is the conclusion that can be reached from a careful and objective examination of his writings.[2] It is an unusual conclusion since, while the role of religion in Nietzsche's thought has been stressed by several commentators, as much cannot be said for the uniqueness that he attributes to Christianity. This uniqueness is certainly of a negative order in Nietzsche's view but it carries so much weight with him that he is compelled to return to it again and again with increased intensity, up to the illusory catharsis of *The Antichrist*, which will require our particular attention.

Nietzsche's absolutely extra-ordinary vision of Christianity was first stressed by René Girard, who also stresses the singular collective blindness—as in the case of Poe's *Purloined Letter* or rather of Andersen's naked emperor—that has afflicted nearly all of Nietzsche's interpreters. As always with Girard, his comments debunk and give a fresh direction, exploding so many commonplaces about Christianity *and* about Nietzsche that he has been largely ignored, and the situation at present can hardly be said to have entirely changed. Thus there is a double censorship—of the real Christian message and of the real significance of Nietzsche—and it is the more difficult to overcome because Nietzsche himself plays an active part in it in all respects.

Girard's interpretation is far from being complete or completely satisfactory, however it sets out along a highly arduous path but one of great fascination, a real challenge to exegesis that the present essay intends to take up in the hope that someone may notice its force, its pure and simple capacity to explain facts that have been systematically ignored because they are hard to deny. It is true that the entire *corpus* of Nietzsche's writings seems to oppose itself to any attempt of the kind, and to mock every effort to reduce it to an unambiguous message, to a real and recognizable content, the more so if the attempt is accompanied by something like cognitive and ethical motivation. And what is it that Nietzsche proposes if not to go beyond all ethics and every normative and objective vision of reality, expressed in a consciously scintillating style, a siren song that appeals to so many readers? The bewildering variety of guises and attitudes adopted by Nietzsche would seem to justify not only the definition given by Gianni Vattimo of "thinking of difference" [*pensiero della differenza*][3] but also the systematizing reaction of Martin Heidegger, who peremptorily declared that Nietzsche's philosophy was "no less consistent and rigorous than Aristotle's."[4] The two positions are not in fact mutually exclusive; indeed, they are cross-referential, sharing a desire to remain in the philosophical sphere (no matter whether 'postmetaphysical' or 'postmodern'), and hold that the answers to the questions raised by Nietzsche cannot, in any case, be formulated in different language. The religious problem and the problem of the Christian anomaly that Nietzsche raises are passed over in silence.[5]

The idea of an essential comparison of Nietzsche's work with religion and with Christianity is still further counter to the main stream if we apply it not only to his thinking but to his life as well. Despite, or rather because of, the masquerading, not to say histrionics, of the author of *Zarathustra*, few other thinkers reveal such a close and even catastrophic connection between

their life and their ideas. The multiplying of disguises, posturings, and statements of intent are evidence of a systematic attempt to flee from identity
rather than of having overcome any prejudice about identity. Disguises are
adopted, above all, by people with something to hide.

Besides taking an author's texts as a whole or trying to fit them into the
procrustean bed of a personal philosophy, there exists another possibility,
supremely hermeneutic and well-known to real psychologists and real readers: to choose only those elements in a text or set of texts that appear as a
sign or indication of what lies beneath. This is a more perilous strategy and
requires having a nose for the hunt and long hours of searching but it is the
only way to capture the richest prey. Once the tracks and signs have been
found, the whole mass, which appeared to be settled and classified once and
for all apart from some shadowy patches normally ignored or declared to be
irrelevant, starts to move and come to life again: we begin to understand not
only what the texts are saying but also, and at times it is the essence, what the
texts do *not* say. I think we hold the key so that all those elements that at first
seemed to confute the unorthodox interpretation come to confirm it, now
that they are explained and set in a broader light, and take on a different even
opposite meaning.

However, with an author like Nietzsche, things are by no means simple.
He makes valiant efforts to put us off the scent. So we need to be determined
if we are to capture Proteus, the Greek god of metamorphosis; we must not
be distracted by his continual transformations but remain firmly convinced
that they result not from strength but from fear, from a desperate desire to
avoid capture. The metamorphosis, the performing, is really a way of escape.

We will look immediately at some concrete applications of this kind of interpretative key. In one of his last works, *Twilight of the Idols*, Nietzsche puts
some important questions in the form of aphorisms:

37
Do you *precede* the others in the race?—Are you like a shepherd? or an
exception? A third possibility is that you are fleeing . . . *First* case of conscience.

38

Are you serious? or only acting? Someone who represents something? or
the thing itself that is represented? In the final analysis you are only the
imitation of an actor . . . *Second* case of conscience.[6]

In the two aphorisms, the desired alternatives are mixed with the feared
(the "shepherd" and being "serious" with fleeing and the fiction of theatre)
as well as the disturbing intermediate "exception"; lastly comes the image
that describes Nietzsche's game here, "the imitation of an actor," that is to
say, not simply masquerading but its inner principle: the performance of a
performance, a formula multipliable to infinity, which is also suggested by
numbering the 'cases of conscience.' We are already told the essential as long
as we distinguish the projections (the "shepherd," being "serious") from what
are authentic descriptions ("fleeing," "acting") and provided that, through
the ambiguous role of "an exception," we discern the will to confuse the two,
the illusion of confusing them ("the imitation of an actor").

Two other images that are just as important in Nietzsche's writings are
the clown or the tightrope walker. In *Ecce Homo*, in the chapter entitled *Why
I Am a Destiny*, he even goes so far as to say: "Perhaps I am a buffoon . . . ,"
however—he adds—for that very reason, a buffoon in whom the truth itself
speaks.[7] This paradox is put more directly in the preparatory outline for the
chapter: "God or clown—this is involuntary in me, this is me."[8] "This is me"
indicates that the imitator of an actor is neither of the alternatives of the
dilemma but their simultaneous possibility, their paradoxical co-presence
that is not consciously decided ("this is the involuntary part in me"), yet
expresses the force at the origin of Nietzsche's will, a lacerating, divided force
that is ineluctable: the imitator would like to be God but he sees himself cast
in the debased role of a buffoon. In the conclusive version the feared alternative is preceded by a "perhaps" ("Perhaps I am a buffoon . . .") and immediately afterwards provocatively proclaimed with an absolute affirmation of
identity, of truth: ". . . my truth is *tremendous*: because until today *lies* have
been called truth." This crazy claim to identity is the last act of simulation;
the long struggle between the God and the clown reaches the stage at which
the two identities are set spinning around, substitute one another and merge
to form a tragic caricature of a divinized clown, of a clown-God.

The texts quoted above should already indicate the strategies and stratagems resorted to by their author. If we are to seize Nietzsche as he rotates faster and faster in his roles and identities, we must *take* him absolutely literally at some points, at certain key moments in his works, that is, surprise and capture him in the literal expression of his thoughts, if it is true, as Roberto Calasso observes in talking about Nietzsche's later works, "genius is also the capacity to take oneself literally."[9] Such a statement should not discourage but indicate that the chase is bearing fruit. The presence of direct traces that can be distinguished from everything else is a clear sign that the prey is close at hand. What must the fugitive do? If he cannot erase his tracks completely (and how can he, since he wants to act a part, to demonstrate something?), he must contrive matters in such a way that the real tracks are taken to be false ones, and the false tracks real. Nietzsche is exemplary here, and the majority of his readers have fallen into the trap. He is to be interpreted metaphorically where he ought first to be taken literally, and interpreted literally where he ought not to be. The systematic nature of the deception rules out any factor of chance.

All this demonstrates that what is at issue here is not merely textual. It would be hopeless if it were just a question of formal elements set *side by side*. But the textual method equal to the task, going beyond Girard thanks to Girard, can be defined as supremely hermeneutical because it draws on the pre-interpretative foundations of any authentic interpretation, that is, on the reality that *generates* the text, while the text follows or obstructs this reality according to how it reacts, according to the position, the vital needs, and the fatal contradiction at the origin of the text. Nietzsche's theatrical metaphors should never be taken as an end in themselves but as a development of the archaic metaphors of combat, hunting, and pursuit, of what the exegete must do if he wants to capture his textual prey. And, in the end, the chase is not a metaphor but real action that presupposes the existence of real prey; and the more important the chase, the more dangerous the prey becomes and as well-armed as the hunter. Taken to its extreme, the fight becomes an *aut aut*: either the prey is captured or it captures the hunter. There is nothing academic, nothing ornamental, in great texts, in great authors. Our relationship to them is one of life or death, of winning or losing, and if you have anything to do with them you can suffer the most bitter and humiliating of defeats, which is to be made captive without knowing it, imprisoned in a cage that

we mistake for the truth, in a fiction that we mistake for reality. Whatever
applause we might receive from this cage can only intensify the silence of our
disillusion when it becomes clear that the enigma has not been revealed at all,
that the enigma itself has caged and swallowed up the unwitting interpreter.

Between the two solutions of capturing or being captured, of devouring
or being devoured (and of controlling the representation or being controlled
by it) there can be a thousand intermediate points in the course of the pursuit, and Nietzsche has the habit of settling on any one of these intermediate points, but not without rapid feints in either direction. The author who
defined himself as "the imitation of an actor" is the most difficult kind of prey,
a predator familiar with all the mimetic tricks to avoid being made a prey
himself, and who knows that attack is the best defense at certain moments;
this is a prey marvelously well-equipped to catch the unwary hunter. But,
leaving aside for a moment the images of the chase and the theatre, what
are the actual extremes between which this strange hunter-actor struggles
to climb, trying to hit and run as he goes? Is there really a dramatic dilemma
between devouring and being devoured, between acting and being 'acted,'
being played by one's own role?

We have seen that Nietzsche would like to be God rather than a clown
but we have also seen that he is unable to divorce the hoped-for alternative
(God) from the one he fears (clown), and resorts to confusing the roles in
an attempt to pass off his fiction as the truth. The dilemma is more than psychological or theatrical, it is religious. Nietzsche has an acute perception of
the ambivalence within what we call religion, and he tries to resolve it in one
final opposition, for him conclusive. The term 'religion' actually describes
two things that could not be more opposite, more irreconcilably hostile in
Nietzsche's view: the god that he invokes more than any other, Dionysus, and
the god that he detests more than any other, the biblical God, especially the
God of the Gospels.[10] It would not appear to be good hermeneutics to reduce
to a single generic common denominator principles that, for Nietzsche, were
infinitely opposed, and this applies to those interpreters like Heidegger—
and their number is legion—who have chosen to ignore the opposition as
irrelevant from a speculative viewpoint. Nietzsche's contraposition can be
overcome only by demonstrating the lack of any objective grounds for it,
but it is precisely this that his interpreters usually fail to do; they usually
take the matter to be already decided one way or the other, with no need

for any particular justification. One thing is never done: to raise the query of whether by chance, at this very point, Nietzsche was not right, at least in part. But to answer that question, we need to investigate what lies behind these opposites, that remain irreducible for Nietzsche, and it is here that Girard with characteristic intuition enters the investigation.

One aspect is at once clear: Nietzsche is the mirror image of Girard in many respects. It is no exaggeration to say that Nietzsche explicitly denies or turns upside down the value of everything that Girard has investigated, from imitative or mimetic desire to Christianity, but one should add that the way in which Nietzsche does it is quite unique, and could not fail to elicit a response from Girard in the form of his stealthy, tenacious pursuit. The strategy adopted by Girard to confront Nietzsche might be compared to a whale hunt: long interminable periods of waiting, relentless exclusion of details that occupy so many other scholars and few but well-placed pitches of the harpoon, in other words, a few studies spread over the years together with a lengthy series of allusions and references in other works. But once again metaphors from hunting can be usefully developed, transformed and set in motion: the image of a whale hunt is well-suited to Nietzsche himself in the first place, and at this point the symbolism of the most metaphysical hunt in modern literature, which occurs in Melville's *Moby Dick*, comes to our assistance, perhaps not perfectly suited to Girard's attitude, but well-suited to describe the voyage I want to undertake starting from his approach to Nietzsche.

Ahab's whole life is obsessed with the white whale; tormented and yet filled with admiration, he pursues Moby Dick to the ends of the earth until it finally drags him down to the bottom of the sea. The hunter and the hunted are the two poles between which Nietzsche oscillates but their contraposition is ultimately an illusion, that is, it is reversible, transitory: in the course of a chase that divides and unites them indissolubly Ahab and Moby Dick come to coincide. The union of the diptych that they have always formed reveals an abyss of evil, the self-destruction of the spirit of antagonism and revenge. Nietzsche also moves between these two extremes, and in the end they unite fatally against him. Is this then the sense of the contraposition made between Dionysus and Christ? Certainly it is the interpretation that Nietzsche wanted to give of the opposition that summed up all others for him, but if this were a *completely* correct interpretation, Nietzsche would not have reacted to the Christian message so angrily like someone whose sport is being spoiled. Evidently Christ disturbs, breaking into the game of the killer who is killed, of the hunter who becomes hunted, of the God who is at the same time a clown, and for this reason Nietzsche was to try to attach to Christ the second term of the alternative in *Ecce Homo* ("God or a clown"), with truly fearful results.

The rules of Nietzsche's game, that subsequently became the rules of a great many of his followers, allow us to understand why Girard is neither able nor willing to follow them to the letter. The polemical tone of his analyses suggests a comprehensible defensive attitude. He does not want to become a hunter in the violent sense of the word, to make an unwholesome reality of an ancient cognitive metaphor, even though this implies the second-level violence of a fierce polemic. With his cognitive motivation and his very prudence he teaches us that our position should rather be like Melville's in *Moby Dick*, whose intention is to describe and recount the chase and the fatal union of pursuer and pursued. More than anyone before him Girard perceives that Nietzsche is great even, perhaps above all, in his errors. This is no less true if we consider that a terrible fate was laying in wait for those who, like Nietzsche, wanted to maintain such errors come what may, wanted to play their game to the bitter end. A significant part of European society (and subsequently, we should add, of the world as a whole), like the crew of the *Pequod*, was to be wrecked along with the theorizer of the will to power.[11]

The relationship of Nietzsche to Girard's investigations is thus not simply one of negation, since if that were the case there would be no reason, from the viewpoint of a mimetico-sacrificial inquiry, to involve ourselves specifically with him. Nietzsche's singular quality is that he has the courage, the temerity even, to take a close look at what he wants to destroy, and as a result his endeavors become an eloquent, dramatic demonstration of what he wanted to deny. Nor is it hard to understand why this should be.

Nietzsche would like to be the ever-elusive prey in this deadly game, the white whale that can never be caught but, if that were really so, nobody would follow Nietzsche; the game, the chase would confute itself. The whale actually corresponds to the ghostly, hidden desire of its pursuer. Nietzsche's problem is that he is condemned to be Ahab, the mad captain who will not relinquish his prey because it is already a part of himself and yet wants to kill it so that it will not be a part of himself, the pursuer who pursues himself, the killer who kills himself. No parable (truly, a parabola) of human existence was ever more bitterly instructive.

In spite of its incompleteness, or rather thanks to the drastic selection of its themes, the path of research initiated by Girard is potentially so rewarding, and could tell us things that have never been said before, at least not with this concreteness or degree of involvement, that it would appear necessary, even urgent, to follow it up, expanding and developing it to its full consequences. As we shall see, the Nietzsche-whale who is Nietzsche-Ahab still has a vital spot to hit, that is, to describe, a spot so sinister and critical that it can reveal the last instant of rebellion, of guilt, and bring us to the very threshold of madness as Nietzsche is about to cross over. In him, suicide, collapse, and final wrecking are not simply mental but primarily spiritual. To watch this happening means taking part in it, to a certain extent; it means embarking on the same ship, and saving yourself only if you realize that it is a dream, a dream bad but grandiose, made of the same "baseless fabric" as "the great globe itself" according to Shakespeare in *The Tempest*.

Our position, our role, can be the same as Ishmael's, the seaman who barely survives the disaster and so lives to tell the tale.

CHAPTER 2

The Eternal Recurrence
of Madness

Once the right key to interpretation has been identified, Nietzsche's own writings and documents about his life provide what seems to be almost overwhelming confirmation, compelling us to see his ideas and fate with fresh eyes. To start with, there is the conclusion that set the tragic seal on his life, and that the 'good' will of many interpreters has vainly tried to minimize: the mental breakdown that occurred at Turin around the end of 1888 and the first few days of 1889.

In a fascinating and well-documented study *La catastrofe di Nietzsche a Torino* [*Nietzsche's Catastrophe in Turin*] Anacleto Verrecchia shows that the old explanation of syphilis as the cause of Nietzsche's madness, an explanation endorsed besides by the authoritative voice of Thomas Mann, is without any factual basis, either medical or biographical.[1] Mann, a writer who took Nietzsche as his much-admired model, is a good example to show us the tricks and the rather obscure ends that have helped to foster the syphilis legend. The strategies set up by Mann to give credit to the rumor display a clear desire on his part to manipulate the data. Nobody was more suitable than the author of *Der Tod in Venedig* [*Death in Venice*] and *Der Zauberberg* [*The Magic Mountain*] at exploiting the turbid nuances of disease and erotism to mingle elements of truth with hagiographical idealizations, manifestly drawing on the maudlin unrealistic biography put together by Nietzsche's sister, Elisabeth Förster-Nietzsche, for commemorative and promotional ends.[2] In an essay published in 1948 Mann made free use of a story about Nietzsche recorded by his friend Paul Deussen: the episode tells of a "youth, pure as a young girl [*rein wie ein Mädchen*], all spirit [*ganz Geist*], all doctrine, all candor and shyness" who is unwittingly brought by "a sinister messenger of destiny" into a Cologne brothel and suddenly finds himself (and here Mann quotes Deussen's actual words) "surrounded by half a dozen figures covered by veils and frills, who looked at him full of expectation."[3] The angelic youth just manages to save himself from these diabolical figures by sitting down at a piano, but—the writer adds—he was to remain marked by a "trauma," that a year later—and this is the arbitrary passage—led him to repeat the experience in earnest, and so caused him to contract the fatal infection. His imagination was never to be free of this trauma, which testified to "his saint-like sensitivity with regard to sin" but caused "a manifest easing of the brakes" to progress secretly within "a mortified sensibility," to borrow Mann's elegant euphemism. This reconstruction is worthy of a master of the *décadence*, and recalls certain brothel scenes in Proust, only that here Mann stops short of a Proustian desacralization: the disintegrating sensibility remains but it is made to depend on external, diabolical factors. While commemorating Nietzsche, Mann was too acute an observer to be unaware of the presence of morbid forces in the philosopher, and yet, in his desire to uphold the romantic myth of the pure, virtually spotless, hero, he very skillfully mixed real elements with invented interpolations. The episode could have affected Nietzsche's repressed erotic imagination, and it is a fact that he had very serious, insuperable problems with women; however the real cause, as we shall now see, can be traced to the way in which he understood his relationships to others: that was what was really morbid in him. Mann made use of the syphilis story with more convincingly infernal results in his last great novel, *Doctor Faustus*, where the main character has syphilis and changes the angelic young pianist into a restless avant-garde composer, who is prepared to make a pact with the devil in order to invent the twelve-tone row.

Like all myths, the syphilis story has been manipulated in a great variety of ways but they all have one aim in common: to deny or cover up a bothersome fact. At the beginning of the last century support for the story came from the positivist psychiatrist Julius Möbius, whose aim was to demolish the entire Nietzschean conception; then it was accepted by Mann and many others with the opposite aim of showing that the causes of the philosopher's madness were accidental and external to the authentic core of his ideas. Surely, the period of latency of this nineteenth century version of AIDS was extremely long since it apparently gave Nietzsche time to write all that he wanted, all the works essential to establish his fame?[4] The 'luetic' school of thought, though it still stubbornly persists, has suffered a decline; what seems to prevail now, without the merits and evocative ambiguities of a Thomas Mann, is the irrepressible 'minimalist' tendency which, as one might expect, minimizes the matter, as if Nietzsche had waited till the end of December 1888 to show clear signs of mental instability, an absurd thesis that simply exposes the use of the previous thesis in favor of Nietzsche.

But before considering the beginnings of his insanity, we might well take a look at its tragic conclusion. A great many of the myths that have built up around Nietzsche's fate can be exploded once and for all by close analysis of some of the documents concerning his madness, brought together and examined commendably by Verrecchia. It may not make very happy reading but, by way of recompense, it is highly instructive.

For a start, it must mean something that Nietzsche's various friends or ex-friends were mostly not surprised to receive his notes and letters of madness (the so-called *Wahnzettel* and *Wahnbriefe*[5]) and to learn of his final insanity, although many of them could not have imagined such a terrible end.[6] But what underlay the relationship of these friends to the philosopher, who was on the point of being consigned, literally in a straitjacket, to his already posthumous fame, was a conniving and hypocritical refusal of reality, well exemplified in Peter Gast, an ill-treated but faithful follower whose mediocre compositions Nietzsche had grotesquely attempted to compare to the music of Wagner. When Nietzsche in his madness wrote to him: "To my maëstro Pietro. Sing me a new song: the world is transfigured and the heavens rejoice. The Crucified,"[7] Gast replied:

> They must be great, those things that you are proceeding with. Your enthu-siasm, your health and everything that you, *a pure body and a consecrated mind* [*reinen Leibs, geweithen Sinns*] have done or can be imagined to have done must rouse even complete invalids: you are contagious health; the epidemic of health that you once wished for, the epidemic of your health

must come. The invocation of the *Crucified* only reached me at Berlin. The weather wears a terrible aspect; the air is cold, smoky, oppressive, an invitation to suicide rather than to a dance [...].

The premiss is not as exciting as the Dionysiac ideal would like to imagine, and provides a telling clue of the existential angst and the alternating states of mind common to Nietzsche and his admirers. In spite and because of that angst the close of the letter confirms the exalted tone of the beginning:

Full of happiness and joy for your triumphs, full of veneration.[8]

This reply shows dramatically that failing to understand Nietzsche's madness amounts to sharing it to a certain extent.[9] What does "failing to understand" mean in a case like this? Gast appears to be in no hurry to enjoy his master's "contagious health" by going to Turin, where Nietzsche had more than once begged him to join him. Evidently the "epidemic of health" suggested the idea of other more real epidemics, to be exact, the contagious epidemic of collective violence that the Greeks called the Dionysian *mania*. Without even admitting it to himself the philosopher's fervent follower retreats in the face of this unconscious specter. He pretends not to understand that the Nietzschean dance set in opposition to suicide can be the best preparation for it, or that "the invocation of the *Crucified*" is a clear cry for help, and already divinizes the master, as in ancient sacrifices: "*pure body and consecrated mind*" (Gast's emphasis), "full of veneration." In other words, the canonization process for Nietzsche will soon be under way.

Nietzsche's fate lies carefully buried under inviolable layers of postmortem admiration, a piece of hypocrisy that has long deserved to be exposed, for over a century now. Too many books and too many ideas have been infected with it, and not to see it really means surrendering to the deep gloom of spiritual suicide. European and Western culture was inclined to commit this suicide of the spirit and is still far from coming to its senses. Turning now to the "epidemic of health" that was able to arouse such insane enthusiasm, we will look at the real nature of the "dance" that might well serve as its emblem.

Another friend, the atheist theologian Franz Overbeck, who appears strikingly apathetic in the face of the abundant signs of mental imbalance coming from Turin, was finally obliged to go there when Jacob Burckhardt, with the condescension that he had always displayed towards the author of *The Birth of Tragedy*, showed him a long and delirious letter from Nietzsche.[10] What must have been the most incredible scene witnessed by Overbeck once he arrived in Turin has been recorded for us: "Among his close friends afterwards, Overbeck also mentioned a spectacle that had presented itself to him in Turin, 'that embodied most horribly the orgiastic idea of sacred furore, such as was the basis of ancient tragedy.' Probably it consisted in ecstatic dancing with erect phalluses."[11] At last the dance so often invoked by the philosopher had been performed. Unlike his future interpreters, Nietzsche was too well acquainted with ancient Greece not to know of what Dionysiac dances consisted.

Before we go into the anthropological implications of Nietzsche's self-destructive investigations, we need to look more closely at the final outcome of his Dionysiac madness; this corresponds so precisely and pertinently both to his life and his philosophy that we must exclude any merely psychiatric explanation, let alone a 'syphilitic' one. Nietzsche's mind broke down in Turin between 1888 and the first few days of 1889 but it continued to emit messages that we can pick up and interpret, a little like the radiation surviving from a supernova, from an exploded star.

After an eventful journey, his friend Overbeck managed to have the now insane Nietzsche admitted to the mental hospital in Basel, on January 10, 1889. The following passage from the *Krankenjournal* [*Clinical Journal*][12] of the clinic reads like a summary of Nietzsche's life and fate:

> His mother's visit visibly cheered the patient; as she entered, he went towards her, embraced her cordially and exclaimed: "Ah, my dear, good mother, I am very happy to see you."—
>
> For a long time he dealt with family matters quite correctly, until quite suddenly he exclaimed: "Behold in me the tyrant of Turin" ["*Siehe in mir den Tyrannen von Turin*"]. After this exclamation he began talking confusedly again, so that the visit had to be interrupted.[13]

Nietzsche's megalomania remained fixed where it had last manifested itself, in Turin, the city where he finished *The Antichrist*, which suggests a new starting date for it, September 30, 1888, the day on which he brought that brief work to a close. Elsewhere the clinic's journal records that the patient kept asking to eat and often sang and shouted at the top of his voice.

A few days later he was transferred to the asylum in Jena, where he remained from January 18, 1889 to March 24, 1890.[14] The *Krankenjournal* describes his movements in these terms: "When walking, the patient jerks up his left shoulder spasmodically and lets the right shoulder hang down. He turns round unsteadily."[15] Other passages in the same document[16] allow us to make connections with Nietzsche's life and ideas that are both precise and equally revealing:

> 19 January. The patient enters the department amidst much polite bow-ing. With a majestic step and with his eyes on the ceiling, he goes into his room and expresses thanks for the "splendid welcome." He does not know where he is. One moment he thinks he is at Naumburg,[17] the next at Turin. He gives correct information about his personal details. His facial expres-sion is confident and self-aware, often self-satisfied and affected. [. . .] As regards content, there is a surprising scattering of ideas in his chatter; from time to time he talks about his great compositions and sings snatches from them; he talks about his "legation councilors and servants." He pulls faces [*grimassiert*] almost incessantly while talking. His chattering also goes on almost incessantly at night. The patient eats mightily.
>
> [. . .]
>
> 3 February. Smeared with excrement [*Kot geschmiert*]. [. . .]
>
> 10 February. Very noisy. Often angry outbursts with inarticulate shouting and no external reason.
>
> [. . .]
>
> 23 February. Suddenly starts 'kicking' another patient [*Versetzt plötzlich einem Mitkr. 'Fußtritte'*]. "Last of all I was Frederick William IV."
>
> [. . .]
>
> 10 March. Ravenously hungry. Always identifies the doctors correctly; for himself, one moment he is the Duke of Cumberland, the next the emperor etc.
>
> [. . .]
>
> 27 March. "My wife Cosima brought me here."
>
> [. . .]
>
> 1 April. Smeared with excrement [*Kot geschmiert*]. "I ask you for a dressing

gown for radical redemption [*zur gründlichen Erlösung*]. I had 24 prostitutes with me last night."

[...]

5 April. Urinates in his boot and drinks from it [*Uriniert in den Stiefel und trinkt den Urin*].

17 April. "They cursed me during the night; they said my mother had wet herself; they have devised dreadful plots against me."

18 April. Eats excrement [*Ißt Kot*].

19 April. Writes illegibly on the walls. "I want a revolver if the suspicion is correct that these dirty deeds and attacks on me are being done by the grand duchess herself." [...]

16 May. "I'm being poisoned all the time." [...]

16 June. Asks repeatedly for help against torture at night.

[...]

2 July. Urinates in the drinking glass [*Uriniert in sein Wasserglas*].

4 July. Breaks a drinking glass, "to protect access to himself with broken glass."

[...]

14 July. Smeared with excrement [*Kot geschmiert*].

16 July. Smeared with excrement [*Kot geschmiert*].

18 July. Filthy with urine [*Urin gesalbt*].

[...]

6 August. (He has) rubbed excrement on his leg [*Ein Bein mit Kot eingerieben*].

14 August. Again very noisy. [...] Drinks his urine again [*Trank wieder Urin*].

16 August. Suddenly broke some window panes. He claims he saw a rifle barrel outside the window.

[...]

20 August. He puts excrement wrapped in paper in the drawer of the table [*Legt Kot in Papier gewickelt in den Tischschubladen*].

[...]

10 September. Drinks urine again [*Trinkt wieder Urin*].

[...]

2 December. Claims to have seen some completely mad little women during the night.

9 December. Vomit. No mistakes detected in the patient's diet, but he often bolts his food.

14 December. Drinks the dishwater [*Trinkt Spülwasser*].[18]

Nietzsche is now a demented wretch, who repeats the most degrading actions in an apparently senseless mechanical way. Great care is generally taken not to look too closely at these documents, and in effect it only seems possible to peruse them with a sense of pity and profound dismay. But they deserve to be examined, and not just to bring us face to face with the sad reality hidden beneath the whited sepulchers of our cultural mausoleums. Here the remnants of what was once the philosopher's personality can be recognized. This is the ground level of behavior, where the structure that was previously hidden becomes visible, now translated most literally into gestures and delirious rituals. Most striking at first is the greed for food and drink together with the obsession about solid and liquid excrement. This is the translation, the monstrous 'reification' of Nietzsche's megalomania, of his desire. This desire has long been at the critical stage defined by Girard as "metaphysical" or "ontological" desire; at this stage desire becomes so intense that it transfigures and divinizes what it desires, making the subject's very 'being' absolutely dependent on it.[19] In the next few chapters we shall examine the causes of such a convulsive inflation, but for the moment we should note how Nietzsche's exploded desire has been reduced to 'divinizing' bodily signs, objects, and functions. Nietzsche has to assimilate a great quantity of matter to expand his own being; he has to swallow, to ingest the Being in which he feels lacking. The obvious physical consequence is that his body expels what he has eaten and drunk, and so the more matter the subject expels with his excrement the more he must eat and drink, and the more he ingests the more he is forced to evacuate. Two aspects of this circle, of this excremental 'symbology,' require to be noticed.

Defecation and urination are, in the first instance, a sign of the power of the subject, the power of the superman. In his posthumous fragments Nietzsche describes a man who beats his horse and then urinates on it (this is a significant image and I shall come back to it at the end of the essay);[20] in another fragment some dwarfs try to attack a giant who threatens to urinate on them. The giant symbolizes the superman-philosopher but at this point it has become a caricature ("When a giant makes water, it's like the Flood"[21]).

However, we find the power of Nietzsche associated with defecation in reference to Wagner, in the places where with heavy irony he accuses Wagner of blocking up his digestive system, and alludes to a consequent need to "liberate himself."[22] By defecating, 'freeing himself' in every sense of the term, Nietzsche imagines that he can expel Wagner and at the same time submerge him in the most degrading and humiliating manner, a double annihilation, physical and symbolic, which we shall analyze more fully when we look closely at Nietzsche's dramatic relationship to the composer.

But in the manifest definitive bleakness of the mental hospital, all real control had gone, and the inflated evacuation revealed the other side of pathological megalomania. If food represents life and power, evacuation represents loss and death. This death could not be accidental because the whole monstrous mechanism was brought into being by a threat that the subject was doing his utmost to avoid, shouting in anger, kicking, and parrying weapons aimed through the windows. Food itself became the vehicle of death, and was systematically poisoned ("I'm being poisoned all the time"). This, then, was a case of murder, and the repetitive, pervasive character of the plot presupposed a whole persecutory apparatus, a group intrigue, a lynching. Such reactions were favored by the conditions in which the patient found himself, and by the climate of apotropaic brutality characteristic of psychiatric institutions,[23] but that only served to highlight certain experiences and dynamics that had been present in Nietzsche's life and mind for a long time. Evacuation had at first carried degrading and grotesque meanings; now it became the failure of food, demonstrating the inanity of its purpose, the real poison taking away its ontological effectiveness, and turning it into its opposite. The only solution therefore was for Nietzsche to reabsorb into himself the Being that had abandoned him, that is, to eat his own excrement and drink his own urine. Like a snake that swallows its tail, the philosopher of the eternal recurrence had to devour himself to demonstrate his own absolute existence.

Nevertheless, not even this circle degraded and reduced to its lowest terms could last. It contained the seeds of its own defeat because its origin was not the fullness of Being but its absence. The excremental circle thus had to expand continually, to embrace ever vaster segments of reality. It was a continuous threat, became the cursing of himself and his divine nature, and reached the point of slandering his mother, saying she had lost her precious urine ("They cursed me during the night; they said my mother had wet herself"), which was equivalent to the expulsion, the cancellation of her son. Nietzsche therefore had to protect himself with almost sacramental forms, to sprinkle urine and scatter excrement over himself to provide a magical protection; to break the glass from which he drank to defend himself from sudden attacks; to vomit and expel his food since it was poison but was then compelled to eat faster and faster to prevent 'someone' from meanwhile poisoning the source of his Being; he even drank the dishwater, which can be seen as corresponding to the excrement and urine of other people; and deposited his own excrement in the table drawer with a sort of ritual. Symbolically this comes close to the funeral rites that Nietzsche liked to attend in the first stages of his madness; in his last letter to Burckhardt he imagined himself as present at his own last rites.[24] It is as if he buried himself in order to be reborn, in order not to die: how can you be dead if you are in a position to attend your own funeral?

Nietzsche was both god and victim, king and human reject. He expressed thanks majestically for a splendid welcome, and at the same time was subjected to continual conspiracies; he was duke, emperor, tyrant of Turin, and at the same time a punctilious courtier and a child seeking its mother's protection. Only sacrifice can offer a thorough explanation for the co-presence of these opposite characteristics in Nietzsche's 'divinization,' and reconstruct their precise sequence that, in his madness, he went on repeating mechanically, in senseless rotation. He was both sacrificer and sacrificed, the performer of the rite and the one transfigured through it to become divinized. Nietzsche requested "a dressing gown for radical redemption"; such a very personal item of clothing, which may be linked to his bodily and ontological functions, became the ambiguous garb of king, priest, and victim.

The sexual references ("twenty-four prostitutes," "completely crazy little women") represent the continuation and culmination of power symbolically expressed through excrement and food. In his derangement Nietzsche became obsessed with the erotic desire that he had never managed to fully satisfy all his life: on the journey to Basel and when he was first hospitalized there he kept asking for women to be brought to him.[25] What could be a more typical substitute for ontological power than sexual power?[26] This sexual-ontological power immediately points us in the direction of Wagner and his wife, Cosima: earlier, in a variant of *Ecce Homo*, Nietzsche had written that he considered her marriage to Wagner amounted to adultery.[27] His clinical file records the very next phase in this delirium when Cosima has become his wife in all respects. The radical nature of this identification testifies to the extent of the forces behind it.

Before pursuing our investigations with further texts and soundings, let us try to 'conclude' this question of madness. Have I perhaps exaggerated my analyses and succumbed to the seductive risk of over-interpretation? Quite apart from the fact that any over-interpretation could only be salutary after so many decades of anemic and opportunistic 'under-interpretations,' it appears to me that the internal consistence of my reading, and its organic ties in every detail with all that we know about the philosopher, are clear evidence that it is not 'over the top.'

Fortunately, a rule exists to help anyone with a genuine cognitive desire to explore the enormous bulk of Nietzsche's writings: they contain a host of clues and often confirm sensationally interpretations lying far outside the realm of a philosophical respectability that has falsified and concealed the ideas of this exemplary best enemy to himself. For a start, we might cite, also in the light of the references to 'intestinal liberation' from Wagner, the paragraph in *Ecce Homo* in which Nietzsche declares:

> Far otherwise is my interest in a problem on which the 'salvation of man-
> kind' depends much more than it depends on some theologians' curiosi-
> ties: the problem of *alimentation*.[28]

In an oblique and contorted way, this statement is perfectly sincere and justified: the "'salvation of mankind'" represents the salvation of Nietzsche himself grappling with the insoluble problem of his ontological alimenta-tion, a problem that was to lead to his final self-destruction. And the conclu-sion of the paragraph is equally illuminating:

> All prejudices come from the intestines. A stone backside—as I have
> already said once—is the real *sin* against the Holy Ghost.[29]

The "prejudices" are the obsessions soon to overwhelm the writer. The "stone backside" was the most unforgiveable of sins, the supreme wrong, because it blocked definitively the entire circuit that guaranteed life and power to an individual who was now breaking down. The sin against the Holy Ghost was, moreover, what Nietzsche frantically circled around in *The Antichrist*, and around which his fate was played out. This was not a case of theological questions concealing alimentary ones but rather of alimentary metaphors concealing theological and spiritual questions crucial to the life and mental balance of the aspirant antichrist.

However, at certain points we can actually glimpse the unconscious development of the philosopher's most arduous concepts. The connection, which is as pathological as it is precise, is with a typically Nietzschean obsession, the eternal recurrence. Many connoisseurs of the philosopher will be thoroughly scandalized and tempted to rend their clothes, and yet, in order to justify their disquisitions they have been obliged for over a century now to ignore facts and texts that speak for themselves.[30] Nobody would want to deny the penetrating philosophical, anthropological, and religious insight of Nietzsche's intuitions, and indeed his perceptions will be explored here more thoroughly than in any orthodox postmodern interpretation, but it is precisely the pathological origin of his obsessions-ideas that made them so penetrating, so effective and in the end so destructive. It is not a question of dismissing Nietzsche's concepts with a psychiatric diagnosis, as Möbius and others tried to do, but rather of understanding the reasons underlying his conceptions *and* his psychic disturbances: the psychic disturbances are only the manifestation of something that neither psychiatrists nor philosophers are willing to see. All Nietzsche's ideas arose from a state of morbid excitement, and were fostered by 'madness' that was present from the start and perfectly recognizable within him, at the heart of our so-called normality. In a late fragment we read the following explanation of the world understood as a cycle of the eternal recurrence:

> *The new conception of the world*
>   1. The world subsists; it is nothing that becomes, nothing that perishes. Or rather: it becomes and it perishes, but it has never started to become and never ceased to perish—it *preserves* itself in the two things . . . It lives on itself: it feeds on its excrement [*Excremente*] . . .[31]

"It feeds on its excrement . . ." This text comes from the spring of 1888. A note to the Colli-Montinari edition is right to cite the fragments on the eternal recurrence composed at the time of *The Gay Science*[32] but the present writer considers it far more useful to consult the clinical records from a few months later, not to reduce Nietzsche to a psychiatric type but to observe the truth emerge in all its stark reality, a truth long denied, feared, and expected. In the final analysis, Nietzsche's eternal recurrence, the secret that he spoke of with trepidation and only to his closest friends, coincides with the premonition and invocation of madness, invoked by the philosopher and sadly fulfilled in himself.[33]

To complete the sinister, painful image vainly hidden beneath the eternal recurrence of a certain philosophical mentality, we need to think about the last period of Nietzsche's madness spent in his sister Elisabeth's house, when he was reduced to a "living trunk and a dead soul," who occasionally made visitors shudder with his outbursts of animal-like howling.[34]

This icon of suffering and degradation requires us now to look into the causes that led to it. What created and fostered the eternal recurrence of Nietzsche's madness, the madness afflicting whole generations that have not wanted to see it?

CHAPTER 3

The Philosopher and His Double

A Crushing Rivalry

Girard helps us to understand the concrete, recognizable answer to the question of what caused Nietzsche's mental breakdown: his madness, the madness of modern man is rivalry that remains unresolved.[1] Nietzsche went mad because of the basic assumptions underlying his life and thought, and the symptoms of nervous instability can be clearly traced in his earliest writings, not to mention the evidence of his letters and other testimony. Sadly, they are symptoms in which we can see a reflection of ourselves. Nietzsche's mind broke down as he rashly attempted to surpass and reject the imitative models that are at the basis of our existence as human beings. Nietzsche was an insecure and highly ambitious intellectual with terrible complexes, both moral and physical (he was, for example, extremely nearsighted all his life), and he was never willing to accept his own imitation, his desire, and the most important mediator of that desire, Richard Wagner, whose extraordinary personality he first encountered and venerated as a young man. Little by little, however, he came to hate Wagner and attacked him for the rest of his life.

The history of their relationship is one of gradually developing rivalry that grew until it became dramatic and insatiable, and even pursued Nietzsche over the threshold of his insanity. Numerous passages might be chosen to illustrate this; we have selected a passage from *Ecce Homo* where Nietzsche describes how his *Human, All Too Human* crossed in the post with *Parsifal*, which is a tendentious figment of his megalomania. This was written at the very end of 1888 when his insanity was about to become definitive:

> This crossing of the two books—it sounds ominous to me. Doesn't it sound like two swords crossing? Anyway, that's how we felt about it: because we both kept quiet.[2]

The obvious comment to make here is that while Nietzsche kept quiet at the time he then went on to do nothing but write against Wagner in a compulsive, obsessive manner, up until his last days of relative lucidity. In the quotation he transforms the two books into swords, which really signifies that he felt *Parsifal* as a deadly threat and intended to fight Wagner with the precise aim of killing him. The image suggests an evenly matched duel, a hand-to-hand fight to the bitter end.

This is not simply a literary image but a revealing symbol. Duelling and what it represented had long been present in Nietzsche like a mania. An episode from his early days at university in Bonn well illustrates this: after encountering another student and having a friendly, scholarly conversation with him, the young Nietzsche quite suddenly, and with extreme politeness, challenged him to a duel precisely because he found him particularly likeable.[3]

The episode gives a good idea of the pathologies of rivalry that were already affecting Nietzsche's mind. He was incapable of making a distinction between the impulse towards friendship and the impulse to mortal combat: the more he felt inclined to one, the more he was compelled eventually to feel the other, a perverse reciprocal effect that could only end badly. Only a really powerful trauma could have caused such distortion, and the event that naturally suggests itself is the premature death of his father Carl Ludwig, a Lutheran pastor, who died of a brain tumor when Friedrich was not yet five years old.[4] The lack of a father was rendered still more devastating by the dull-minded, petty bourgeois environment of his childhood.

In the last of a series of unfinished autobiographical sketches made as an adolescent, Nietzsche wrote of his anguish at being left "orphaned and abandoned."[5] Besides feeling abandoned, nothing is more likely than that he felt himself to be mysteriously to blame for it as well. Immediately after the account of his father's death he describes a nightmare that he had at that time: a ghost comes out of his father's tomb, takes up a small indistinct figure in its arms and draws it back into the tomb; Nietzsche interpreted this as a premonition of the death of his younger brother who died suddenly from convulsions the next day. Whatever is to be made of the episode, it seems obvious that the child who is led back to the tomb by the ghost of its father is recognizably Friedrich in the first place, suggesting a further sense of guilt on his part because his younger brother died instead of himself.[6]

The child Friedrich was 'found guilty' by his father; this enigmatic sentence without appeal must have created a profound, deflected rancor in Nietzsche which can be detected, as well as his struggle against the sense of guilt, in his writings, in the unrealistic idealization of his parent and in his polemical attitude to so many things connected with the milieu of his father and family, his attitude to religion for a start. All these impulses and feelings in Friedrich were subjected to deadly meticulous repression, vainly interrupted by a few written fragments: nothing was to express or give voice to the deep needs of this child emotionally abandoned to his own devices.

The rancor and compressed anguish erupted dramatically in 1862 in a literary fragment *Euphorion* where a ghostly figure goes in search of its double in order to section its head; the last part adopts the technique of a horror story to describe how the character is suffering from tabes dorsalis.[7]

Nietzsche's behavior in regard to this brief but brilliant literary creation further indicates the dominance of self-repression in him and the devastating effects on his fragile psyche of the effort that it involved: having sent the story off to a friend he at once repented, and in another one of his letters defined the story as a "repulsive novella" and a "monstrous manuscript" [*Monstrum-manuscript*], ending with a disturbing remark: "When I finished writing it, I broke into diabolical laughter [*diabolische Lache*]."[8] This kind of laughter already suggests the laughter of madness. The momentary lapse of self-censorship provoked reactions of a dissociative nature that were immediately punished by rejecting the text, which meant coincidentally condemning its author. It was Friedrich who felt himself to be "repulsive" and "monstrous,"

and who confirmed throughout his life the tabes dorsalis that ends the fragment. Later he wrote to Paul Rée: "so far I have been an isolated monster,"[9]
and in some letters written in the last period before his patent madness he
signed himself "the monster."[10]

Nietzsche's relationships to his father and his family have not formed
part of Girard's inquiry, in part because they go beyond the essential situation that he wants to draw our attention to, and perhaps he also wants to
avoid any dangerous confusion with explanatory schemes of a Freudian type.
However, it is easy to see that Nietzsche's sorely-missed paternal figure was
not the Oedipal rival of some absurd incestuous desire but a figure to love
and be loved by whose radical lack was felt by Friedrich: the ambivalence of
love and hate comes after, and not before, abandonment by the father.[11] The
trauma is not so much fully explained by its origin within the family as given
its initial orientation by it. Unfortunately, once the structure of the trauma
was fixed Nietzsche transformed it into the cardinal principle of his relationships to other people. As a result his psyche was introverted, burdened with
complexes, and pathologically reactive.

On the basis of these assumptions we can imagine what must have happened
with Wagner. There were previous father figures to whom Nietzsche attached
himself—his philology teacher Friedrich Ritschl, the historian Jacob Burckhardt—but the author of *The Ring*, born, incidentally, in the same year as
Friedrich's father, summed up and surpassed them at one go to become the
one real putative father of the rancorous, anguished orphan, sparking off all
that was best and worst in the younger man's painful, conflicting emotions.[12]
For his part Wagner, of illegitimate birth (as Nietzsche unkindly reminds us
in *The Case of Wagner*[13]), must have recognized certain similarities to himself
in Nietzsche who, moreover, possessed the academic qualifications and culture that he lacked.

We can hardly overestimate the influence of Wagner—the prestigious figure addressed by the young Nietzsche as *Pater Seraphicus*, as his
"mystagogue,"[14] the "mightiest of all spirits" beside whom he was "only the
future"[15]—on the young professor from Basel as he grew to maturity. The
intuitions about tragedy and its Dionysian character, the perception that
the violent foundations of the drama are somehow connected to the violent

foundations of culture, and the comparison with Christianity were all matters that Nietzsche began to study and develop while he associated with the great composer. In the end, however, the relationship to Wagner and its decisive influence provoked a disastrous reaction from Nietzsche, the first signs of which can already be detected in his writings favorable to Wagner. This led eventually to a complete break with his old friend, his impossible father.

Certainly the tyrannical, hyper-mimetic Wagner was the most unsuitable person to establish a well-balanced and proper relationship. A ruthless exploiter of all those around him, he manipulated other people and especially their money, not only in questionable taste but often dishonestly; yet Wagner, who was capable of putting the Bavarian state finances at risk, was as hard to resist as a hurricane, and compensated for his enormous defects by the power of his music and by his generosity to friends as well. It is typical of his style, for example, that after a lifetime of hurling unrepeatable abuse at the Jews, both in speech and in writing, he accepted the devoted friendship of a young Jew who was so distressed when the composer died that he took his own life.[16] With his shyness and complexes, the young Nietzsche could not help but feel dominated and crushed by such an exuberant personality, sufficient to furnish him with a whole series of traumas far superior to the trauma of the Proustian brothel so skillfully fabricated by Thomas Mann. "It is as if he were trying to resist the overwhelming effect of Wagner's personality," Cosima wrote in her diary in 1871,[17] showing great perception but undoubtedly she did not realize how serious the situation was for their young and eccentric friend, nor perhaps did she imagine or give much weight to her own close involvement in it.

Nietzsche's imitation of the model that he had at first admired but gradually came to oppose went so far as to vie with it in the field of music, the field in which it excelled. As a result Nietzsche suffered a series of bitter humiliations, making himself appear ridiculous in the eyes of Wagner and Cosima, who were certainly not very kind even to composers who were as good as the theorist of the music of the future. A single sentence from Cosima's diaries shows us their opinion of Nietzsche in this field: "We are little vexed by our friend's music-making pastimes [die musizierende Spielerei unseres Freundes], and Richard expiates on the turn music has taken."[18]

Whatever the value one puts on Nietzsche's music, it can stand no comparison at all with his philosophical works. However, the history of

his attempts to gain attention for his music can be reconstructed through
various episodes, the most traumatic of these was the reception given to his
Manfred-Meditation when he sent it to the great conductor and Wagner
expert, Hans von Bülow. This was on July 20, 1872 just after he had heard
von Bülow conduct *Tristan and Isolde* and had experienced its "healing
strength," as he wrote in the accompanying letter.[19] Von Bülow replied on
July 24, 1872 practically by return of post, in a vein of unforgettably savage
criticism:

> . . . your *Manfred-Meditation* is the most wildly fanciful eccentricity, the
> most disagreeable and anti-musical thing in the way of notes on scored
> paper that I have set eyes on in a long time. I have had to ask myself several
> times: is it all a joke, was your aim perhaps to parody the so-called music of
> the future? Are you aware of it as you blithely go on breaking all the rules
> for connecting sounds, from the highest syntax to ordinary orthography?
> Leaving aside the psychological interest—since one perceives an unusual
> spirit in your feverish musical product, a distinct spirit in spite of all the
> aberrations—your *Meditation*, from a musical point of view, is equivalent
> to a crime in the world of ethics [*in der moralischen Welt*]. I have not been
> able to discover a single trace of the Apollonian element: and as to the
> Dionysian element, quite frankly, I was compelled to think of the morning
> after a bacchanal rather than think of that. If you really do have a passionate
> urge to express yourself in the language of sounds, then it is indispensable
> to acquire the first elements of the language: imagination floundering in
> an orgy of remembered Wagnerian sounds is not the basis for production.

And after a stinging comparison with Wagner, von Bülow concludes:

> Once again—you are not to take it badly. Besides, you yourself defined
> your music as "horrible"—in fact, it is, and more horrible than you may
> credit; that is to say, not ordinarily damaging, but worse: damaging to
> yourself, who could not have found a worse way of killing even an excess of
> spare time than to rape Euterpe in this fashion.[20]

Von Bülow, who had lost Cosima to Wagner and been ejected from Wagner's circle after a degrading and scandalous *ménage à trois*, must have vented

his spite on the amateur musician who was still a friend of the composer. The letter reveals quite clearly the bitterness of the husband rejected by Cosima Liszt in favor of the genius who was capable of realizing her ambitions. Von Bülow therefore seized the opportunity to revenge himself on someone who appeared even less equal to the situation than himself.

The fact that Nietzsche delayed replying until the last days of October shows how keenly he felt the blow, and the letter that he drafted is of the greatest interest. There is a nauseating profusion of apologies and thanks in the sugary, hypocritical tone that renders much of his youthful writings so hard to digest but also makes us very much aware of the deadliness of his education. However, he lets slip some extremely important admissions when he comes to describe his feelings while composing:

> Well, thank heavens I had to hear this very thing from you. I know already what an uneasy moment I caused you, and in return I must tell you that you have been very useful for me. [. . .] . . . sometimes I am overcome by such a barbaric urge, such a mixture of obstinacy and irony, that I fail to perceive—just like you—what is to be taken seriously in recent music and what instead is to be regarded as caricature and sarcasm. Among my closest acquaintances [. . .] I passed it off as a satire on official, established music. And the original name for the state of mind was *cannibalido* [sic]. With that, it is unfortunately clear to me that everything, with this mixture of pathos and malice, undoubtedly corresponded to a real state of mind and that while I was composing I experienced such enjoyment as never before. Some sad conclusions can be drawn from that about my music and, even more, about my states of mind. How can you describe a state in which plea-sure, disdain, arrogance and sublimity are mixed together? Now and then I fall prey to such dangerous moods as those. However, I am far, infinitely far—and you must believe this—from judging or evaluating Wagner's music on the basis of my semi-pathological [*halb psychiatrischen*] musical excitement. I know only one thing about my music, that it enables me to keep control of a state of mind that would perhaps be more dangerous if it was left unsatisfied.
>
> And at times, in this tormented state, I too thought better of this music: a truly deplorable condition from which you have now rescued me. Praise be! So this is not music? Well, I am very lucky then, I need no

longer concern myself with this *otium cum odio*, with this really odious
way to waste time. What is important for me is the truth: as you know,
it is more pleasant to hear it than to speak it. I am then doubly in debt
to you.[21]

Nietzsche's admissions about "semi-pathological musical excitement"
with which he is enabled "to keep control of a state of mind that would
perhaps be more dangerous if it was left unsatisfied" are really alarming,
and tell us much about the balance of his mind already in those years. This
state of mind is described as "*cannibalido*," no doubt a slip of the pen for
cannibalitudo (cannibalism),[22] and it is manifestly the same spiritual state as
when the young Nietzsche burst into satanic laughter at the conclusion of
Euphorion. That he was "infinitely far" from evaluating the music of Wagner
on the basis of his own music defines his precise problem at that moment: a
far cry indeed from the "healing strength" of *Tristan*! The fact that Nietzsche
wrote the *Manfred-Meditation* against two artists that he particularly loved
and admired, Schumann and Byron, presents us with the same dynamic as
the duel in Bonn, and it allows us to sense the intensity of the love and hate
that he nurtured against the real target of the piece, the ex-rival of von Bülow.
If we consider this tortuous stratification of models-rivals, the point of the
attempted maneuver when Nietzsche sent his composition to von Bülow
becomes quite evident: he secretly hoped that the conductor would want
to take revenge on the man who had stolen Cosima from him. And some
suspicion of the maneuver probably prompted the conductor's swift and
merciless reply. Nietzsche's mean-minded, unwholesome attempts to give
vent to his inferiority complex were all repaid with interest. The description
of his furious outbursts of composing as *otium cum odio* is unequivocal: the
Latin phrase has the same alienating effect as nineteenth-century medico-
sexual terminology[23] and indicates here the radicalizing of an incurable
rivalry. Nietzsche tried to hide the growing intensity of a sentiment that was
destroying him, and erase the sordid memory of the maneuver that had just
failed, with outrageous hyperbole, thanking his savage critic for actually saving him, and redoubling his thanks in the name of a truth that it would be
"more pleasant" to hear than to speak.

Thanks, however, to a sense of decency that sometimes came to his
rescue *in extremis*, Nietzsche rewrote the draft immediately afterwards and

dropped nearly all of the above from the letter that was actually sent. The description of his states of mind was toned down, apart from a symptomatic "diabolical irony," and only the close, though concealing even more, allows some greater sincerity about his reactions to filter through: "You have been of *great help* to me—and to confess as much still causes me a certain amount of pain."[24] So powerful was the trauma that his mind as it broke down was still attempting to metabolize its memory, presenting *Manfred* in *Ecce Homo* as a work about which

> Hans von Bülow had said that he had never seen a musical score anything like it: and that it was the rape of Euterpe.[25]

And at another point, referring to another one of his compositions—a *Hymnus an das Leben* [*A Hymn to Life*] with a poetic text by Lou Salomé—he let slip a phrase that sounds almost like a cry from the heart: "Perhaps there is greatness in that passage, even in my music."[26]

Nietzsche's failure as a composer was bound up with his parallel lack of success in the erotico-sentimental field. Clear and convincing evidence has come to light, in the studies made by Verrecchia and Fini, that Nietzsche was affected by what would nowadays be called impotence, an impotence not without overtones of homosexuality, which can easily be the result of a situation of total failure with women.[27] In this field, too, comparison with Wagner was doubtlessly very painful for Nietzsche, since Wagner was a great lady-killer, not to say man-killer, his conquests including the companions of the male members of his circle. Far from arousing redoubled gratitude in Nietzsche, the savage criticism from von Bülow, in his role as great conductor as well as husband and betrayed friend, must have been doubly devastating for him. We should not forget that the *Manfred-Meditation* was the amended version of a no less disastrous composition that we have yet to consider, the *Nachklang einer Sylvesternacht* [*The Echo of a St Sylvester's Night*], with which Nietzsche undertook quite absurdly to replace Wagner in Cosima's eyes. After von Bülow's demolition of the *Manfred-Meditation*, Wagner appeared to triumph twice over and in two different roles, as a musical genius and as a lady-killer.

Defeat as an artist introduces the most seriously unsuccessful aspect of Nietzsche's existence, confirming his incapacity to realize for himself any kind of sentimental life worthy of the name. His emulation of Wagner in the field of art was a clumsy approach to possessing an object of affection. At its core lay Nietzsche's secret love for Cosima, a sentiment cultivated in silence, an impossible and suppressed passion that persisted into the dark world of madness and, all the indications suggest, was of an intensity proportionate to Wagner's enormous influence. Never was a lover less likely to succeed: even if Cosima understood the tempestuous feelings that she had aroused in her husband's introverted and argumentative friend (and it seems improbable that her feminine intuition could fail to understand them), it is easy to imagine the reactions of such an arrogant and calculating woman, who had at last picked the 'winning horse' in Wagner, the genius that she had longed for; and who, when her father Liszt died at Bayreuth, would make no changes to the festival program.[28] From such a situation Nietzsche must have emerged emotionally burnt out. He was never to pluck up enough courage to take the initiative with a woman, and experienced a string of failures or rather of humiliations, which were poignant or pathetic, depending on one's point of view. In the world Nietzsche inhabited, every male must know how to play the savage game between the sexes if he is to attain the goal of copulation but it is a game that all official morality and pedagogy regard as not needing to be taught, and nobody was ever naturally more ill-equipped to play it and more certain to lose than poor Nietzsche.

Nietzsche fell in love with Cosima for the same reasons that he wrote his music: to draw close to the idolized and envied model, to dislodge him and take his place. He did not spend Christmas 1871 at Tribschen where he had been cordially invited. His biographer Curt Paul Janz analyzes "the motive for the painful renunciation" thus:

> ... the previous year Wagner had surprised and delighted Cosima with the composition of the *Siegfried Idyll*; this year Nietzsche had gone back to being a composer and placed under the Christmas tree his *Echo of a St Sylvester's Night* a piano piece for four hands, to be performed with Cosima.[29]

For Nietzsche the Wagners had become a kind of adoptive family but Nietzsche stayed away this Christmas, the first of a series, one of many hellish Christmases that were to mark his bachelor existence. Wagner himself was offended by his friend's standoffishness but, as we can infer from anecdotal evidence, the couple could only ridicule the *Echo of a St Sylvester's Night*, and Nietzsche came to hear of it.[30] It is hardly surprising that the Wagners noticed his "growing tendency to express himself polemically and apodictically."[31] Nietzsche reacted to these continual checks—checks, we may note, that he eagerly sought for himself—with increasing tension. This is also apparent in his notes made at the time where the music of his adversary is grotesquely underrated,[32] which gives a hint of the break to come.

The *coup de grâce* was delivered to Nietzsche by Wagner's triumph at Bayreuth in 1876. Nietzsche hoped to find himself at the center of attention on account of his just published fourth *Untimely Meditation* on Wagner (a wearying exercise in sycophancy occasionally interrupted by hatred). Instead, he found himself pushed to one side in the great Wagnerian junketing, ignored and outclassed by the composer who was too busily engaged with the colossal undertaking that he had set in motion to think of other things.[33] The real conflict that we have to imagine between the two men is not one of subtle psychology or philosophical ideals but a brutal, elementary clash between the weak, neurotic Nietzsche who was in love but obliged to remain in the shade, and the egocentric, super-dynamic Wagner, who was not only enveloped in the greatness of his music but was enjoying the homage of the leading figures in German and European society. The reaction of rivalry in Nietzsche is strong enough to cause him real physical malaise. His biographer Janz, who certainly cannot be suspected of antipathy towards the subject of his monumental study, makes the following general comment: "Often, following psychic shocks, his body took refuge in illness by means of some accident piloted by the unconscious"[34] and, referring particularly to the Bayreuth festival, Janz describes the eloquent contrast (and connection) between Nietzsche's visible sufferings and the general excitement of the moment,[35] in spite of his attempts to find more generous explanations for the philosopher's malaise. When Nietzsche went to Bayreuth he was plagued by splitting headaches, terrible migraines that would only leave him on the brink of insanity, and whose origin was psychosomatic; he left feigning to be bored by the music but then returned saying that he was unable to stay away; finally he withdrew once and for all, ignored by Wagner and to the great relief of Cosima.[36] From then on, Wagner and all things Wagnerian, the whole of Germany itself, were to be made the constant object of the philosopher's polemics.

The Impossible Death of the Rival

This concentric series of emotional and existential defeats meshed with what have been defined as "inferiority complexes in facing life":

> At the time of his relations with Wagner, these unhealthy tendencies could only be strengthened by the overpowering friendship of that most tyrannical of geniuses and by the emotional defeat that Nietzsche suffered through his undeclared and unrequited love for Cosima. Added to these, there was his scanty success as professor at Basel and the sense of bitter humiliation caused by the general indifference that later greeted his books on publication. With the exception of a handful of friends, little or no attention was paid to him.[37]

These are fundamental observations; however, they become misleading if, as is usually the case, they are given strictly biographical value, a reductively psychological significance. Something far different is involved here. If what happened to Nietzsche ceases to appear as a pure individual accident but instead is seen to be the manifestation of general, recognizable laws, then its significance is no longer psychological or, to be more precise, psychologistic. What we have before us, then, are objective forces that concern our nature as human beings, and are basic to our being men and women, and basic to what we understand by psychology. Girard uses the term "anthropology" to designate this objective level, a level which is habitually ignored, and he has identified an immense force within our anthropological reality, the force of imitative or mimetic desire, that in my view can be equally constructive or destructive according to how we use it.[38]

What we become and are is due to our imitation of various models but since when we imitate a model we want to possess the same things—material or symbolic—that the model possesses, the relationship, which is in itself extremely fertile, can degenerate into rivalry. In Nietzsche's case he had every inducement to imitate the model of a much-admired genius, Wagner, and the result was a typical three-sided situation, in which the model (Wagner) unwittingly indicated to the imitator (Nietzsche) what he was to desire (fame as a composer and love for Cosima). And it was in the sphere of physical, sexual love that Nietzsche's imitative desire emerged most ingenuously and disarmingly. All his life he sought laboriously and futilely to fix an erotic object of desire through a model, desperately replicating triangular situations that could never have worked out happily, in view of his incapacity to control the deadly dynamics of rivalry.[39]

The most spectacular instance of triangular desire, pursued by Nietzsche in contorted ways almost completely out of touch with reality, was the "trinity" that he thought to set up with the honey-tongued Paul Rée and the formidable but charming Lou Salomé, who once told a protestant minister a few years after bringing turmoil into his life: "I cannot live according to a model and I could never be a model for anyone else."[40] Such trinitary romanticism, a caricature of the mimetic dependence that it denied, could only bring resounding defeat on Nietzsche.

Against this background of clumsy unsuccessful maneuvers, it is significant that Nietzsche's favorite opera was Cimarosa's *Il matrimonio segreto* [*The Secret Marriage*], an authentic comic apotheosis of triangles with everyone falling in love imitatively with everyone else. Nietzsche's admiration for the opera was so great that his lackey, Gast, set his libretto to music; and in fact, only something as irresistibly infectious as the amours of Cimarosa's masterpiece could have carried away the neurotic, emotionally blocked German professor. Idle speculation, however. It is hard to imagine anybody further removed than Nietzsche from the sublime, mimetic irony of the eighteenth century, from the spirit of Goldoni and Mozart.[41] Only one thing corresponded to his situation: the metaphysics of adultery unrolling through a river of sound in *Tristan and Isolde*, but the musical and erotic potency of Wagner's music overwhelmed him and made it clear that adultery with Cosima was both necessary and unrealizable.

The Nietzschean triangles are a sad and rancorous illustration of the worst possible outcome of imitative relationships. In fact, their triangular configuration can easily lead to *envy* in the imitator, especially if the model is domineering and voracious in his self-centeredness, as in the case of Wagner. Envy is not simply the desire for what someone else possesses but is a feeling of radical deprivation of something that, because it belongs to the admired model, ends by appearing to be indispensable to life itself, to the individual's identity. The envious person thinks of himself as the victim of the greatest injustice, an injustice that deprives him of the light of the sun, of his right to exist and love, and he will do everything in his power to possess the secret that makes the other person so inexplicably and undeservedly superior. At this stage ontological and metaphysical desire begins to collapse, and we have already seen its terminal breakdown in the tremendously literal symbolism of the clinical reports on Nietzsche.

'Envy' is a highly reproachful term, a mark of infamy applied to those who appear envious in a world of the 'unenvious.' It can be one-sided:[42] Cain envied Abel without the least fault or envy on Abel's part. But the world in which we live is not normally composed of innocent Abels but of countless Cains, who often go undetected simply because they are better at pretending. Envy is more relational and mimetic than anything else, since what it triggers off among men and women is mimetic desire. And even when it is one-sided, it comes of an imitative relationship that has malfunctioned in the past, and 'taught' the envious one how to envy. From a symbolic point of view, Cain learned to envy from his parents who were guilty of following the wrong model, the serpent, in envying God; and for that sin they were driven from the garden of Eden.[43] Mimetic relationships between men easily consist in mutual envy, and—worse still—in a mutual grounding in envy. The imitator often (not always) envies the model because the model is already thinking in those terms, seeing his role as a possession to be jealously guarded. This was, in substance, the situation that came to exist between Nietzsche and Wagner, even if Wagner undoubtedly lived through it in all innocence, in the sense that he wanted to make Nietzsche an extension of his own greatness. Not realizing the consequences of what he was doing, he only saw his generous friendship repaid with growing hysteria, to his lasting disgust. Everything happened as if they were under a spell, whose causes were beyond the grasp of those directly involved, though with different degrees of responsibility.

Situations of this type have been studied as a form of "double bind," that is, as a contradictory relationship with no way out for the individual involved whatever he does.[44] The imitator is invited to follow and admire the model (the public adoration of Wagner) but as soon as he approaches too closely to the model, he is driven away (Nietzsche was laughed to scorn for his music, as would also have been the case if he had declared his love for Cosima). The model tends to confirm his role, prestige, and superiority but when the imitator retreats in defeat, the model unconsciously but promptly issues another invitation to imitate him in order to maintain his role. The imitator, in short, receives a two-fold contradictory injunction ("Imitate me!"—"You'll be in trouble if you imitate me!") and is consequently 'punished' whether he imitates the model or not. Usually the imitator is unable to resolve this paradoxical situation, since he derives his identity, his Being (the ontological aspect of desire) from it.[45] Fostered by a repressive and bigoted environment, this was evidently the role that Nietzsche's absent father came to assume for him and which, as a young man, he then applied to the duelling episode at university, anticipating the characteristics of the attracting model who because he is attractive *must* be hostile as well. This distorted process, what I have called "the structure of the trauma," continues to be repeated and worsens throughout the individual's life unless other imitative factors intervene to correct it, factors that obviously have to interact with the individual capacity for choice.[46] But freedom of choice diminishes continually within the pathological triangle: the imitator sees his model as increasingly unattainable and himself as condemned by an ineluctable fate to perpetual defeat. While the model becomes circumfused with divine light, his follower sees himself relegated to the shadows, a mediocrity, abandoned and non-existent.

Ontological desire as it appears in relations between Nietzsche and Wagner is well illustrated by the following passage from a letter written on April 18, 1873, that is, some months after the *Manfred* debacle and a few days after Cosima's note about "our friend's music-making pastimes." In this letter Nietzsche tried to repair the sorry figure that he had cut yet again with the Wagners, who were about to transfer to Bayreuth:

> Most Revered Maestro,
>   I live in constant remembrance of the days in Bayreuth, and everything new I learnt and experienced in so short a time now spreads out before my eyes ever more fully. If you seemed dissatisfied with me when I was there, I can understand it only too well but I can do nothing about it, because I am very slow to learn and understand, and then every moment spent close to you is an experience I had never thought about before, one that I wish to

impress on my mind. [...] I beg you to think of me as just a pupil, even with a pen in my hand and an exercise book open in front of me, and moreover as a pupil who is very slow-witted and not in the least versatile. The truth is, I grow more melancholy day by day because I am perfectly aware that I would like to help you and be useful to you in some way but, instead, I am quite incapable of it, not even able to help distract you or cheer you up.

However, perhaps one day I will succeed, when I have finished what I have in hand, that is, an essay against the famous writer, David *Strauss*.[47]

The imitator prostrates himself and grovels before the model, the "Most Revered Maestro," but his exaggerated declarations of inferiority and submission reveal the intensity of desire in its incremental phase, also indicated by his growing melancholy, a state of depression brought on by a sense of inadequacy in regard to the model; at other times Nietzsche reacted to this depression with a cyclical mood of elation tending to megalomania. Unctuously humbling himself to the level of a "slow-witted" schoolboy, Nietzsche had at all costs to demonstrate his own worth to his never-'satisfied' idol; with the dynamics already identified in his *Manfred* and in von Bülow's harsh critical reaction, he could find nothing better than to vent his repressed anger against a polemical target, one to "distract" and "cheer up" his model at last, that is, to lower the ontological tension that condemned the imitator to permanent inferiority. The common enemy, indicated by the maestro, was "the famous writer, David *Strauss*" (note the italics), the unwitting target for the explosive fumes of Nietzsche's first *Untimely Meditation*; the ferocity of his attack on Strauss is even more gratuitous when we consider that Nietzsche, in the schizophrenic manner that is now familiar to us, seems to be taking revenge for the influence exerted on him by *The Life of Jesus* and his fondness for its author.[48] But it is clear that such diversions do not change, but only confirm the problem from which they arise.

How little Nietzsche could trust to maneuvers of this type emerges not only from an internal analysis of his relations with Wagner but also from documents of the same period that show us the strength and gradual intensification of the double bind of rivalry. The rancorous ill-will of the follower of Wagner towards the model whom he felt had destroyed him built up, though he was unwilling to acknowledge it, conditioning his behavior in a way that was plain to see and apparently inexplicable. The phenomenon was becoming uncontrollable. As he wrote to Carl von Gersdorff, not many weeks before the letter that spoke of "a pupil who is very slow-witted":

> I have had some splendid letters from the maestro and Frau Wagner, something has emerged I knew absolutely nothing about, that is, Wagner was very hurt because I didn't go to spend New Year with him. This you knew of, my very dear friend, but you didn't tell me. Now, however, all the clouds have cleared away, and not to have known anything about it has been more to the good, because at certain times there are a great many things that you cannot put right, and there's even a risk you will make them worse. Besides, the Lord knows how often I give the maestro cause to be upset: and every time it comes as a surprise to me, and I fail to understand clearly what it depends on. So I am all the happier that peace has now been restored once more. But tell me your opinion as to the reasons for being repeatedly upset. I really cannot imagine anyone being more loyal to Wagner than myself, in all the important things, and how anyone could be more deeply devoted to him than I am [. . .]. But in regard to minor matters of secondary importance and to my personal need, that I might also call a "hygienic" [*sanitarisch*] need, to avoid too *frequent* cohabitation, with regard to that I must preserve my freedom, really only in order to be able to remain loyal in a higher sense.[49]

In such passages it becomes impossible to understand where deliberate falsehood ends and good faith of a laborious, tortuous kind begins. Nietzsche feigns amazement but, besides having little or no right to be amazed at the reactions to his shabby behavior, he had been fully informed of the offence given to Wagner by a letter from Cosima, in which she went on to say that she was sure that, in time, "the purity of genuine sentiments" would blossom once more.[50] And that was certainly happening, even if it lacked the purity imagined by Cosima. Nietzsche made every contorted effort to hide the truth from himself, attributing to his "very dear friend" the responsibility for keeping him in the dark, but he emerges into the light with the revealing remark that it was better not to know anything "because at certain times there are a great many things that you cannot put right." Nothing could be more unreal and hypocritical than the "peace" about which he declares himself to be "all the happier." The expression "minor matters of secondary importance" betrays his desire to control and minimize them because they are in fact determinant and, as he himself admits, irremediable.

As a consequence Nietzsche had to take *sanitarisch*, 'health' measures against Wagner, whose presence was poison, to be avoided like infection with a contagious disease. To remain "loyal in a higher sense," that is, *in the absence of Wagner*, sounds rather like certain epitaphs: generosity comes no easier than generosity towards the dead since, being dead, they can no longer do any harm. The bittersweet euphemism is to be taken in its real originary sense. The only solution to the problem of Nietzsche's health would have been the death of Wagner, that is, his total destruction. Only this conclusion, taken quite literally, provides a more complete understanding of the scatological image of Nietzsche with his digestive system 'blocked' by Wagner's music. Nietzsche, filled through music with the Being belonging to the admired and envied model, must liberate himself through his own excrement: expulsion-defecation thus means to eliminate the rival, having absorbed his strength; which amounts, in a monstrous manner, to eating him . . . And isn't that what is ultimately implied by the cannibalism referred to in the draft letter to von Bülow?

The illusory liberation through killing the rival seemed to come about some years after the letter to von Gersdorff. On the news of Wagner's death, Nietzsche, who was dejected after the trinity with Lou Salomé and Paul Rée came to an inglorious end, wrote to Gast as follows:

> For some days I have been seriously ill, giving rise to some apprehension
> on the part of my landlord and his wife. Now I feel well again and I even
> believe that Wagner's death was the greatest relief that could be brought to
> me at the moment.[51]

Verrecchia comments: ". . . either Nietzsche was already insane, or he was morally monstrous."[52] When confronted with behavior of this kind a moral reaction is more than comprehensible, and still more comprehensible when we think of the absolute tranquility, not to say amusement, of Nietzsche on another occasion: towards the end of his life he was spending the winter in Nice as usual when an earthquake devastated the city causing hundreds of deaths. His Olympian comment was: "I was the only *merry* person in a mass of ghosts [*Larven*] and 'sensitive souls.'"[53]

However, if our proper condemnation of Nietzsche's inhuman reactions remains isolated, there is a danger that it will project the evil on to the "moral monster" without further investigating the causes of that evil, which lie hidden within each one of us. The nature of Nietzsche's reaction to Wagner's death, at its truest, is suggested by the growing verbal excess, the abuse and insults heaped on his friend even after his death, *above all* after his death, attributing Wagner with the grotesque histrionics that he was trying to distance from himself. If Wagner's death had brought "the greatest relief" to Nietzsche, ought we not to observe an opposite kind of behavior? The fact is that the decease of the rival can make the rivalry relationship definitively irremediable: the rival now becomes totally elusive, the imitator can no longer demonstrate anything to him, the final sentence of ontological, constituent inferiority becomes, as it were, without appeal. Nothing could now soothe the ulcer that plagued the philosopher; no defecation, whether more or less symbolical, could free him.

With reference to Nietzsche's reaction to the death of his maestro and rival, Overbeck speaks of "a truly fearful alternation of states of mind."[54] These alternating states also included an ill-considered attempt to 'win back' Cosima's heart with a letter, something that the composer's widow did not deign even to acknowledge with a reply. Only the drafts of this letter remain, raving in tone.[55] The shade of Wagner, like the ghost of Nietzsche's father and the ghosts that haunt Shakespeare's characters, showed itself to be even more powerful than the real, living Wagner.

The presence of obscure, unconfessed motivation in Nietzsche's lunatic arguments did not go unnoticed by a hyper-mimetic reader such as Gabriele D'Annunzio. While he sympathized with Nietzsche's ideas, he defended the greatness of the "Jesus of Bayreuth." Writing about *The Case of Wagner* in an article in 1893, he observes:

> As the reader can see, there is not only a case of Wagner but also *a case of Nietzsche*. There is something frenzied about this bizarre little book: in its disorderly sequence of ideas, inconsistent syntax, and furious invective.[56]

At this point, it is highly illuminating to compare Nietzsche with D'Annunzio, the leading figure in Italian decadentism, and not only in Italy. Contrary to an oft-repeated critical commonplace, D'Annunzio had

a magnificent understanding of the reasons underlying Nietzsche's thinking, which he had only recently come to know, but he was careful to defend
himself against it: absorbent as a sponge but jealously independent, he
sensed himself to be the possessor of a richer and even more virile ambiguity than Nietzsche's declamatory forays. Wagner was an integral part of this
ambiguity, with the dream of a theatrical neo-foundation.⁵⁷ Nietzsche had
rejected this through envy and hate but D'Annunzio made it his own, even
if it was not without clear symptoms of rivalry. Against the background of
their shared passion for Wagner, presenting the same anthropological and
historical problems, it is D'Annunzio who throws light on Nietzsche rather
than the other way round. D'Annunzio wanted to make use of Nietzsche
without disrupting the ambivalence that was the precious matrix of his art:
he positioned himself not far from the philosopher of the superman, but not
too close either, so as not to destroy the human and artistic representations
that he meant to explore.

   D'Annunzio's mimetic inquiry allows us to understand far better than any
will to power what happened to Nietzsche in his rivalry with Wagner. In his
article D'Annunzio says nothing about the similarity of the "Nietzsche case"
to the situation of characters in many of his novels, including *L'Innocente* [*The
Innocent*] which was published just a year before. The main character in that
book, Tullio Hermil, is morbidly jealous of his wife who has been unfaithful
to him with a famous writer (a clearly ironical reference to the author himself). The image of this Other Man obsesses Tullio, who meets him one day,
emblematically in a fencing gymnasium. When he hears that the writer has
been struck down by a fatal form of paralysis, Tullio is seized by

> a strange desire to laugh [. . .]. It was most peculiar excitement, a bit con-
> vulsive, never experienced before, indefinite. My spirit was seized by some-
> thing like the bizarre, irrepressible mirth that seizes us sometimes amid the
> surprises of an incoherent dream.⁵⁸

The hysterical-type symptom of this "strange desire to laugh" is the same
infernal laughter of the young Nietzsche that was destined to grow longer
and louder as the catastrophe approached, and corresponds to that "greatest
relief" felt by Nietzsche at the news of Wagner's death. However, Tullio's triumph is short-lived. Immediately afterwards, with a degree of self-perception

that Nietzsche never wanted for himself, Tullio realizes that his feelings are the opposite of the specious joy experienced a moment before:

> I no longer felt any joy. All the hatred exciting me had died out. I was plunged into sadness and gloom.—The wreck of that man had no influence on my state, it was no shield against my own wreck. Nothing had changed in me, in my existence, in the prospects for my future.[59]

Tullio realizes that his rival has given him the slip yet again, and this time forever. Rivalry was already present in his possessive, selfish love for his wife; it now appears uncontrollable in his relations with her; she is the rival-partner who was to become the Enemy [la Nemica] in D'Annunzio's *Trionfo della morte* [*The Triumph of Death*]. Tullio vainly seeks a monstrous, tacit alliance with his wife to get rid of the child that she is expecting by the writer, and vainly he brings about the child's death: his awareness of having sacrificed an innocent victim was to give him no peace.

To understand what happens to D'Annunzio's character, Tullio, and to the mind of Nietzsche we must return to the situation that we started from, the duel. The duel, evoked by D'Annunzio and neurotically demanded by Nietzsche, is the typical and traditional image of rivalry; its succession of perfectly symmetrical acts aims to make an ultimate imitation prevail, the most precise imitation, the fatal one, and gives us with the scheme of all rivalries in its most transparent form: the *doubles* relationship, a relationship that can result in utter destruction, in which the Other's "wreck" corresponds to one's own.

In *Daybreak*, writing in a feverish tone peculiarly his own, Nietzsche describes the self-destructive nature of this dismal ritual, that dominated social life of the period:

> *The duel.* I consider it an advantage, someone once said, to be able to have a duel when I absolutely need one; and in fact I have fine comrades around me at all times. The duel is the last entirely honorable way for committing suicide that is left to us, unfortunately it is a roundabout way, and not even completely sure.[60]

Here once more, disguised as "fine comrades," is the fellow-student at university, challenged to a duel because he was particularly likeable. With the added detail of being "entirely honorable" the duelist seeks to establish attention, social prestige, that he feels himself to lack. However, the final goal of this quest—self-destruction—is no less crazy than its basic assumption and, in addition, the "way" to attain it remains "roundabout . . . and not even completely sure." The prime objective should be to kill the hated rival, but the will to fight arises from truly disastrous uncertainty, deepening within Nietzsche like a cavern hollowed out by an underground river in limestone rock. He is afraid to be more precise about the "way" and, in the reassuring isolation of writing, he tries to remove the awareness that he can feel growing dangerously inside him. He wants to remove his perception that the duel is taking place within his ego but he senses that there is no escape: he belongs to it with every single fiber of his being, to the point of suicide. D'Annunzio, once again in *The Innocent*, expresses marvelously well the destructive and symmetrical character of the rivalry double bind:

> . . . it was an enemy, an adversary with whom I was about to engage in struggle. He was my victim and I was his. I could not escape from him, and he could not escape from me. We were locked together in a ring of steel.[61]

The reason why these modern characters, like Shakespeare's Hamlet,[62] cannot vent their violence by duelling, to which they appeal all the time, is because the destructiveness of the doubles in them normally proceeds by more tortuous and insidious routes than the ancient fight to the bitter end. A modern person will not allow himself to behave in a blatantly aggressive way, since it meets with growing social disapproval, and he will often put up a certain moral resistance to his hatred for the model-rival.[63] In modern society it becomes increasingly difficult for the relationship of rivalry to find an outlet in bloodshed as in former times and, unless some other way is found to overcome the difficulty, the relationship inevitably manifests itself within the person as an irresolvable internal conflict between repulsion and attraction, between love and hate.

Nietzsche's short-lived relief at Wagner's death was also an attempt to react to his grief, to deny the problem along with the rival. He hated Wagner as intensely as he loved him, and for the same reasons. This is the Nietzsche who wrote in *Ecce Homo*, in an unguarded moment with something harrowing about it: "I loved Wagner,"[64] and, from his last days in Turin, comes significant evidence of how Nietzsche begged the daughter of his hosts "to play some Wagner for him—only Wagner."[65] Modern society's violence without catharsis[66] shows the infernal nature of rivalry quite dramatically, where there is no access to communicate love and no willing resignation to understand that someone who is admired and loved is not to be hated, let alone killed with impunity.

This explosive cocktail causes the doubles to multiply within the individual; in some cases they can intensify creativity (which is imitative and therefore duplicative) but, in other cases and often at the same time, they can upset mental stability, even seriously, to the point of insanity. In fact, both within the individual and in interpersonal relations, the mimetic doubles tend to form a structure, a *system*. This is richly fertile in creative terms if there is psychological and social control of the system, as occurs with the representative duplications of art but if there is no control the system can literally drive a person mad.[67]

Here, too, D'Annunzio is most pertinent, providing an example of the creative potential of the mimetic doubles. Like Nietzsche, he displayed substantial ambivalence in his relations with Wagner but resolved the doubles of his mimeticism in artistic creativity and in a fascinating investigation into his own desire, first boldly undertaken in *Il piacere* [*The Child of Pleasure*]. In the novel *Il fuoco* [*The Flame of Life*] Stelio Èffrena pursues the dream of a new Dionysian art capable of subduing the "unbounded many-eyed chimera" of the masses, and finds in Wagner his supreme model and rival to be revered and surpassed. But Èffrena-D'Annunzio is more resourceful than Nietzsche and successfully turns to creative ends his desire to see his model-rival off the scene: Wagner is already old and ailing when he arrives in Venice; he collapses and Èffrena, coming to his aid, carries him on his back; at the end of the novel Wagner dies and Èffrena, with some of his friends, is a pallbearer for the Hero, the Revealer, effectively appointing himself as Wagner's successor in dramatic art. Rivalry has not been overcome but skillfully diverted, translated into the derived ritual of art, thus permitting the imitator to relate to the world in a difficult but constructive relationship, making it possible for him to learn and to look at himself. Nietzsche never wanted to exploit these possibilities; we have already seen how he immediately rejected a youthful example of his artistic and theatrical impulses. Such impulses were pushed into the background but, in spite of all, they surfaced later in the works of his maturity. The 'doubles system' that developed in Nietzsche's mind and philosophy, under the initial impulse given by his unresolved rivalry with Wagner and in the absence of the representative diversion of art, certainly turned out to be creative but it remained fatally orientated towards mental imbalance. It is not difficult to demonstrate how these rivalry doubles were the hidden engine driving Nietzsche's thinking.

The Masks of a Philosopher

Nietzsche's real situation, filled with resentment towards Wagner as the embodiment of 'power' in the artistic, sentimental, and social field, has to be recognized as the core of his idea of the will to power, which in fact constantly connotes the will to engage and compete. The will to power glorified by Nietzsche is the positive transfiguration of his own resentment, since it concerns himself, while resentment itself is the insidious, covert will to power that the weak feel towards the strong, the few, the aristocrats:[68] the weak constitute the 'herd,' against whom Nietzsche hurls his thunderbolts with a regularity approaching monotony; they are the shapeless mass who invented morality and Christianity in order to prevail. Because Nietzsche realizes that these are only different degrees of a single force, he attempts to take it over, to gain sole mastery of it. The will to power, that he must possess to the highest degree, is the decisive difference, destined to save him from the leveling resentments of the herd, from the oscillations of the doubles of rivalry.

But to overcome rivalry by overcoming *all the rivals* is an impossible undertaking. We should not let the figure of the superman dazzle us: the superman, or the over-man, as the term is sometimes translated usually in the effort to transfigure its essence, is simply the man who surpasses all others, the one who always wins. This could be the object of an interesting study in historical and social psychology: a description of the countless ways in which the figure of the superman, so improbable in appearance and so disagreeable in substance, came to be glorified and made the subject of subtle disquisitions, where it was often clearly to be understood that the sole representative of this extraordinary species was the speaker himself. In fact, the egos of commentators are titillated by the Nietzschean superman for more sophisticated reasons, but not very different reasons from those of the average man who dreams of becoming *Superman*, or the frustrated housewife with her fantasies of being his faithful companion or a woman endowed in her turn with superpowers. These examples are banal but there is no cause for indignant protest: the popular imagination, in its *sancta simplicitas*, can be more revealing than a thousand learned discourses. With good reason, moreover, Nietzsche did not go into greater detail about his superman, since he is characterized in largely negative terms: the over-man systematically pursues the opposite of what the others do, that is, he is characterized by *negative imitation*, the imitation typical of rivalry relationships. This form of imitation is under the illusion of distinguishing itself by incomparable originality when it really spies obsessively on everything that the others do, with the sole aim of always doing the exact opposite. Des Esseintes, the main character in Huysmans's *À rebours* [*Against the Grain*], finds his most brilliantly bizarre ideas vulgar as soon as they are imitated by the 'shopkeepers'; he is a dandy who must always act contrary to others, the precursor of what current lifestyles show us as mass consumption, the most servile and blind imitation imaginable.

It is fair to recognize that the tragic quality of Nietzsche's creation is greater compared to the images of present-day consumerism, providing we remember that true tragedy is not tragedy that soars high above the everyday world but tragedy that feeds and lives on it, revealing its hidden face. The tragedy implicit in the superman is that this authentic competition puppet must not only beat the herd but must surpass his peers as well, and in fact Nietzsche always projects the superman into a glowing past or a still more luminous future (and later we shall see what is the source of that light) but never into the present. And you can be sure that the superman will always find someone in the present to beat him: Wagner, Wagner's ghost, Wagner's admirers, the whole wide world eventually. There is thus a permanent doubles crisis within Nietzsche's mind. He is too perceptive not to notice it and, at the same time, too blind not to dream of victory, the final victory of the last double capable of destroying all the others. The doubles of the will to power are the problem that has to be solved, but also the means to solve it, and its victorious resolution. The will to power is already madness, with Nietzsche insanely hoping to cure himself using his own means; it is an unreal dream of mental health and divine self-sufficiency, a revelatory delirium of omnipotence.[69]

There is a sincere tone to the expression of Nietzsche's dream, and real poetic qualities. This authentic pathos of desire makes it easier to understand the fascination that his figure exerted over whole generations, nursing their delusion of final victory for their existential longings.[70] How many lives full of frustration and bitterness have not recognized themselves in Nietzsche's hidden resentment, and fancifully imagined taking revenge on the hated 'herd' or on society as a whole? Just before Nietzsche's philosophy came to full maturity, the Russian writer Dostoevsky made an unrivalled analysis of these existences that had something metaphysical about their frustration; dwelling in the underground of their own embitterment, they would later become the "devils" of one of his greatest novels. In the last phase of his life before his mental breakdown Nietzsche read both *Notes from Underground* and *The Devils* but failed to apply their terrible lesson to himself. Not many years would pass before these children of the underground, these "devils," would transform their resentment into demented ideologies, into horrific political regimes.

There is however an important difference between Nietzsche and his imitators, a difference that allows us to grasp the peculiar cognitive relationship that his ideas bear to his unresolved rivalries. Like many of his admirers and like ourselves, Nietzsche refused to see to the bottom of his desire, envy, and rivalry: the sad burden of our experience as human beings.[71] But, precisely when he was concealing his desire from himself, Nietzsche wanted his desperate victory to emerge where he felt the root of the problem lay, that is, in desire itself which he does his utmost to transfigure and utilize in a philosophical disguise. After hiding his face behind a mask, the same mask adopted in a strenuous effort to conceal his disastrous need for models,[72] Nietzsche sought to make it central to his vision, asserting that "All things profound love the mask."[73] But the mask as a symbol and ritual element refers to man's sacred origin; it is literally the image of that origin and so brought Nietzsche face-to-face objectively with fundamental anthropological reality, with what underpins not only the individual but the entire culture and history of mankind.[74] Through the mask, Nietzsche's underground of resentment becomes an archeological excavation, revealing the various strata of his and our cultural unconscious. Aware that what he felt was indissolubly linked to knowledge, visible and hidden at one and the same time, Nietzsche set out to broadcast it to the world, in a venture without precedent that was not only verbal but existential. And it is this that constitutes his characteristic, paradoxical consistency or rather meta-consistency, and gives his works their exciting and yet sinisterly prophetic tone, a prophecy that their author was the first to fulfill. This desire that Nietzsche denied and pursued, this desire-mask, explains his attitude towards Dionysus on the one hand, and Christianity on the other.

For Nietzsche Dionysus is the Greek symbol of the sacrificial foundation of society and culture, but Girard's contribution, in explaining Nietzsche's motives for this characterization shows itself to be valuable, even in its simplifications, because here, more than anywhere else, Nietzsche had to maintain the ambiguity of the mask, of which Dionysus is the god.[75] Contrary to what Nietzsche would like us to believe, the mystery of the mask can be solved; we need only accept it for what it is, not so much a luminous surface as a macabre grave, one that we can and must excavate, containing, like an archeological excavation, not only layers of our psychology but also of our history, of our collective prehistory. If we are to do justice to Nietzsche's greatness, traditional philosophy is not enough; we must resort to a more complex and comprehensive study of mankind, to the anthropological dimension explored by Girard.[76] Nietzsche senses, *knows*, that the secret of human origin is in Dionysus. So it is through the labyrinth of Dionysus that our way now lies.

CHAPTER 4

The Foundation of Dionysus

The Real 'Death' of God

For the purpose of examining the archeological strata uncovered by Nietzsche our starting point must once more be the "double-bind" dynamics of desire, freely developing from Girard.[1] Perennially active in shaping men's lives within the social environment, they make the creation of rivalries and violence inevitable sooner or later, and these in their turn tend to multiply. Nothing is more contagious than violence; every violent action against us provokes violence as an equal and contrary response in a way that is almost irresistible. This symmetrical, destructive imitation can lead to a group crisis, a *doubles crisis*, which represents the original model sparking off the crisis in Nietzsche's mind. The only immediate way out of such a crisis is to concentrate the violent imitation on a single object, whose choice is agreed by all the opposing parties: we have already observed this mechanism at work in Nietzsche's attempt as a young man to show solidarity with his model by verbally killing David Strauss, and also in the case of D'Annunzio's Tullio Hermil when he tries to save his marriage by physically eliminating, with his wife's complicity, the child who is the double of his detested rival. When this mechanism operates within a group, it can easily give rise to a new imitative current that concentrates a growing

53

number of individuals against the new enemy, until the entire community is united against him. This can all occur in a very brief space of time. The enemy with the ability to induce rivals to make common cause is the victim, chosen for any reason, in the end for a random factor, that attracts the attention of the others. He is held responsible by all for what is going wrong and, once chosen, is normally killed or at least expelled from the group. The victim is the 'difference' that makes it possible to put a stop to the proliferation of the doubles; it was this difference that Nietzsche desperately sought in order to block the doubles of rivalry within himself.

The phenomenon of victimary selection exists spontaneously in the form of *lynching* but had already been codified in the very distant past as *sacrifice*, the controlled repetition of collective violence, an essential step—according to Girard's mimetic theory—in understanding the origin of man as a cultural animal, a process that can only take place if it is unconscious. In fact, it is mimetic peace that allows consciousness to develop, not the other way round: the community feels itself to be really threatened by the victim who, through the exponential excitement of the group, acquires the characteristics of a monster. Once killed, the victim is regarded as the superior cause of the miraculously restored peace (Girard's reconciliation transfer, which I prefer to call divinizing, sacralizing, or ecstatic transfer), and adored just as intensely as he was hated before (Girard's aggressiveness transfer, that I prefer to call violent transfer).[2] This is the cognitive 'pit' concealing the victim, becoming, in the course of man's cultural evolution, a real grave in which the victim was buried. Sacrifice explains the origin and nature of the archaic sacrificial divinities that Nietzsche invokes. The sacrificial god is both the sacrificed victim, whose characteristics he takes on, and the god who requires to be literally and regularly 'fed' with further sacrifices. Without these killings the god would die because he is born through the transfigured death of the victim.

As Girard has shown, Nietzsche clearly refers to this process in Aphorism 125 of *The Gay Science*, that contains the famous phrase "God is dead." A perceptive interpreter of Nietzsche, De Lubac, defined this phrase as "the mother cell of his thinking";[3] it puts Nietzsche's plan for sacrificial neo-foundation in a nutshell. Nietzsche's reference is to the sacrificial god who must first die in order to live. In ancient Greece this god exhumed by Nietzsche was Dionysus, a divinity who presided over a sacrificial rite still extremely close to spontaneous lynching. This rite was the *sparagmós*, the dismemberment of a living victim which, in the most archaic version of this collective rite, was one and the same as the homophagy (from *homós*, meaning raw in the sense of alive), the act of devouring the victim's still quivering flesh.[4] The fact that the victim was originally a human being is attested by the history of Greek religion and exemplified in *The Bacchae* by Euripides. This is why Dionysus is the god of the mask: ritual disguise is the means that makes it possible to kill without being recognized and without provoking others to violent imitation, and it translates into concrete terms the concealment that enables the group to close its eyes to its own violence and transfigure it into the *sacred*, a mysterious power that the group then uses to project the violence, of which it is unaware, outside itself through a form of unconscious participation termed mis-knowing or persecutory unconscious by Girard.[5] The mask, the tomb, and this persecutory unconscious have their verbal equivalent in *myths*, stories of persecution transfigured so as to explain what happened as the result of the presence or action of some divine force. Myths, like the mask, are seen and experienced as inexplicable all the time that we connive at their concealed violence.

Nietzsche's various explorations of the sacred foundation of Dionysus, which brought it to interact destructively with his mimeticism, both revealed and concealed this red-hot material. Nietzsche, or if you like, the conscious Nietzsche, was never to completely remove the mask of Dionysus because, in order to do it, he would have had to recognize the real nature of the violence that he advocated, and its origin in his own desire. Revelation and concealment are found in combination in Nietzsche, switching and alternating bewilderingly but in a way that we can reconstruct, as long as we remain unconfused by the typically multiplying doubles of his ideas or by his habit of according the same status to mystifications and discoveries that are equally sensational in nature. And since the double bind that generated his works is basically always the same, its results can already be recognized in his earliest significant philosophical works.

The Promethean Promoter of Culture

Nietzsche's juvenilia clearly reveal his frantically intense efforts to construct a mask to conceal himself using material derived from his dual background,

classical and Wagnerian. Lying latent behind the professorial hauteur, the
excessive high spirits, and the brilliant intuitions there was tension and
polemical passion ever ready to strike, which would erupt uncontrollably
whenever it could with the single aim of annihilating the opponent. There
was something hysterical in all this that foreboded ill for the future, and it
was by means of this morbid enthusiasm that Nietzsche evolved his image
of ancient Greece, far in advance of the fatuous idealizations then in vogue
but it was an image deeply imbued with his own spirit of rivalry. He was
an outstanding scholar but his genius was matched by his bitter resentment,
and in ancient Greece he recognized the impulses that tormented him so
cruelly: man's "most terrible aptitudes" were seen as "natural," "the depths of
hatred," "voluptuous cruelty" in the tiger-like eyes of the victorious warrior,
"the night and horror" of pre-Homeric mythology, strife "as health and salvation," "the cruelty of victory" as the "peak of the joy of living," law developing
"from *murder.*"[6] Envy could not be missing from this picture:

> As regards spite and envy, all of ancient Greece held a different opinion
> from us, and thought like Hesiod who, on the one hand, describes one Eris
> as bad, that is, the Eris who sets men against each other in cruel destructive
> strife and, on the other hand, he praises a second Eris as good, the Eris who,
> in the form of jealousy, spite and envy, spurs men to action, not to destruc-
> tive strife but to *competition.* The Greek is *envious,* and does not see it as a
> defect but as the action of a *beneficent* divinity: what an abyss between our
> opinion and his![7]

The link with Hesiod's *Works and Days* is as ingenious as it is misleading: certainly, competitive as they undoubtedly were, the Greeks sought to
utilize their competitive spirit in a positive sense but Nietzsche's spite and
envy never crossed their minds, nor the hysterical rivalry that he dreamt of
unburdening through spite and envy. Hesiod's good *Eris* (Strife) is ritually
controlled emulation and not some ferocious frustration ready to strike. The
brilliant philologist refused to see the link between, on the one hand, the
spite and envy that he wanted to applaud and, on the other hand, the "cruel
destructive strife" that is its direct consequence and that he tried in vain to
set over against competition. This modern advocate of envy thus felt himself
authorized to come out with statements of the following kind:

> ... we must all agree to the truth—which sounds cruel—of the statement
> that *slavery is essential to culture*: a truth that certainly leaves no doubt as
> to the absolute value of existence. This truth is the vulture that devours
> the liver of the Promethean promoter of culture. The wretchedness of men
> who struggle to live must be further increased to make it possible for a
> limited number of Olympians to produce the world of art.[8]

At other points in the same essay Nietzsche makes it clear that the attain-
ment of this luminous ideal requires us to discard spectral figments such as
"the dignity of man" and, in the name "of *might*, which is always evil,"[9] to
oppose the detested driving forces of democratic money-based civilization,
for which "the only remedy is war, and still more war."[10]

We need to remember in the first place that such aberrant statements
belong to pieces written by a saber-rattling young Nietzsche intent on
impressing the haughty, chauvinistic Cosima with his idea of the community of Olympians devoted to art, amongst whom he should obviously be
included. The idea recurs in his writings and is clearly tinged with compensa-
tion. However, the Olympic vision itself is insufficient to satisfy the lunatic
visionary: the wretchedness of the excluded "must be further increased." This
detail is so striking that it makes one wonder what motivated such ruthless-
ness. But if we remember the contrast between this increase and the "limited
number of Olympians," we at once deduce that it means a continual increase
in the number of slaves and an ever-reducing number of the elect, a little
like the extreme evolution of capitalism according to Marxist theory. The
ultimate phase in this oddly 'capitalistic' evolution of Olympus would thus
find Nietzsche the only one with access to Olympus, to Wagner's home,
and to Cosima, the future Arianna. There is a vulture gnawing at the liver
of the "Promethean promoter of culture," not because he feels distress at the
unhappy fate of the majority but because he fears to end up as one of them,
and he is none other than the lover of Cosima enchained by Wagner-Zeus.
In dramatic form still, the image shows us a victimary situation reversed,
analogous to the situation that Nietzsche experienced symbolically during
the earthquake in Nice in 1888: excluded by Cosima and musical genius, the
world's outcast, the victim who finally has his revenge.

However, this sort of mimetico-sacrificial 'psychoanalysis,' precisely
because it brings out objective anthropological truths, should not lead us to

overlook the serious implications of Nietzsche's assertions. In the passages quoted he says exactly what he intended to say; the tenor of his declarations never changed, indeed it worsened, even maintaining the same mythic imagery: in 1888 he still wrote of the superior beings "beyond good and evil" as having a duty to defeat morality and Christianity: "We believe in Olympus, and *not* in 'Christ Crucified' . . ."[11]

Attitudes such as this were certainly not isolated in the ideological climate of the period and are to be found, fortified by Nietzsche's influence, in D'Annunzio and Thomas Mann. D'Annunzio, who aspired to dominate the 'infinite chimera' of the masses, embraced a dream of nationalistic neo-foundation, while, in his *Reflections of an Unpolitical Man*, Thomas Mann opposes the fragmentizing force of civilization by stating the case for culture in a sacrificial and Nietzschean sense, the *Kultur* that "binds [. . .] without excluding 'bloody ferocity' [*blutige Wildheit*]."[12]

Of course, if we are to correctly evaluate assertions like these, serious in themselves anyway, we need to view them in context but we also need to look at the person concerned for signs of a corrective, of some other element to counterbalance and prevent them being applied with monstrous consistency: often, indeed, inconsistency proves to be the salvation of human beings.[13] Now, while a Christian element existed in different forms in both D'Annunzio and Thomas Mann to influence them and prevent diabolical extremism—and the same can be said for the racist, anti-Semitic Wagner—the case of Nietzsche was sadly different: there was no real, effective obstacle in him to the progress of these insane ideas. There were obstacles but the "Promethean promoter of culture" contrived diabolically to turn them in the worst possible direction. Nothing could stop him, and as a result a great many vultures gathered after his death to devour the "Promethean promoter of culture" postmortem.

To make quite sure of his insane revenge Nietzsche was prepared to rig the evidence systematically, to deny what was as plain as a pikestaff. Just as he deliberately equivocated over Hesiod, trying to justify his envy of Wagner to himself, so he also refused to admit that the authentic nature of Dionysus in ancient Greece was not vaunted openly, but hidden in the mysteries and nocturnal rites. Euripides, exceptionally, reveals something of the god's innermost nature but in a very different atmosphere from the one that Nietzsche imagined. The joyful, spring-like naturalness in which he delighted is nowhere to be found in the culminating scene of *The Bacchae*. It is pure horror still, even though filtered through the disguises of drama and myth. Of necessity, therefore, Nietzsche accused Euripides in *The Birth of Tragedy* of representing the decadence of tragic theatre, that is, of revealing *too much* the mythic mask of tragedy to be able to work, but it is symptomatic that when Nietzsche comes to the horror of the dismembering of Pentheus he fully approves of it as a wholesome exercise and attributes it to a nonexistent palinode by Euripides. For much the same reasons that he showed himself to be unaware of elements in Wagner that were unmistakably Christian, Nietzsche as a young man was reluctant to see Greek tragedy as gradually, partially, revealing the god who gave it origin while telling us of his dangers. In glorifying Dionysus and tragedy Nietzsche tried to evade the collective nature of the god, the identification of Dionysus with the furious mob on the point of lynching, which he describes as "natural instinctive intoxication" [*instinktiver Naturrausch*] and as an unconscious "vernal impulse" [*Frühlingtrieb*][14]: at all costs Nietzsche wants to see Dionysus as an aristocratic divinity, as the tutelary god of his community of Olympians, anticipating—though still with an illusory 'social' hint about it—what was to become his superman. Even at the most mature stage of his thinking, Nietzsche's suggestions about the collective death of the god were powerful but they remained isolated. He tried to fit them into the sacred background of his neo-pagan philosophy, in a way that was apparently aiming to reproduce what occurred in the archaic sacred, where the violence of the group was transfigured and projected into the sphere lying outside the community. Yet this attempt actually turned out to be something unprecedented, a modern way for sacrifice, with a mixture of awareness and attempts to distance its ugliest aspects, clothing them in a 'natural' or 'mystic' background. The main problem was to get round the hidden presence of the Christian revelation, that, for the same reasons that hamper revenge for modern rivals, spoilt Nietzsche's 'game' by bringing it out into the open, showing the authentic nature of the mechanism.[15]

However, before we examine the decisive factor that led to the crisis in Nietzsche's venture, we must understand it in the limits in which he meant to achieve it, straining to keep the real adversary as far off as possible; we need to be clear about the tricks and expedients with which he hoped to succeed

in this impossible undertaking. Without the Christian revelation of the killing of God by men, the phrase "God is dead" would not have the resonance
and meaning that it has. Nietzsche knew this, but at the same time it was the
last thing that he would have wanted to hear, or to admit.

Like the madman in *The Gay Science*, Nietzsche was completely isolated:
far too aware of the collective killing of God to find any relief in group
catharsis, in group purification, his need was still too great for him not
to miss it, not to desire to be rid of his burden of consciousness. What he
describes in the aphorism in *The Gay Science* is a real 'twilight of the gods'
where we can still make out the faint afterglow of ancient sacred fires; however, no alternative appears—the Christian alternative—to be rejected, with
differing degrees of awareness, both by the madman and by nonbelievers in
God. The most pertinent parallel is with Wagner's grandiose *Twilight of the
Gods*, where the home of the gods begins to totter under the pressure of an
inevitable destiny. Have any of the opera's many admirers ever bothered to
look closely at what, at *who*, is the cause of the dissolution, and at what the
love that threatens to destroy Wotan's power signifies? We would do better
to believe, with the connivance of Wagner himself, in the para-religious cult
of Bayreuth or, alternatively, in the enigmatic *vox clamantis in deserto* of a
Wagnerian heretic, of the Nietzschean madman who tried to take possession
of the death of God. The factors motivating Nietzsche's rivalry with Wagner
went beyond the merely psychological and involved the religious and historical environment; and it was for the same reasons that D'Annunzio pursued
his theatrical and national neo-foundation. What Nietzsche had also found
intolerable at Bayreuth was the presence of a *rival cult*, which he tried to
overthrow with the aphorism about the death of God, instituting for a new
cult, a sacrality with no precedent.[16]

The madman wants to incarnate the ancient fire, and holds a lantern,
the last remaining symbol of that fire. While the others continue to live in
the shadow of what has happened and, though they no longer have any gods,
are still protected by the persecutory unconscious from which the gods took
their origin, the madman realizes that it is all an illusion. He decides to take
the initiative and takes up a position in a no-man's-land between revelation
and lies; this precludes him from speaking with authority as someone who
speaks, not for himself, but for the truth and it also denies him the reassuring unconsciousness of those who listen to him without understanding.

He is the sole actor in a drama where nobody else knows the parts, a drama from which Nietzsche would have liked to go on to a sort of meta-drama ("the imitation of an actor") or an impossible persecutory meta-unconscious capable of uniting conscious and unconscious, clarity and concealment. Only the madman, in his isolated pronouncements, his cognitive schizophrenia, could be a 'light' to himself, as he demonstrates in the end when he throws his lantern on the ground and shatters it.

Nietzsche was both the doubles crisis and the divine difference that ought to resolve it. Therefore he had to be god himself, one way or another. If this is a mad proposition, we should however take care not to dismiss it as mere madness since, in the words of Shakespeare's *Hamlet*, there is method in it. The 'method' was the anthropological origin of culture and the sacred that Nietzsche was compelled to repeat and to attempt to renew in order to legitimize his inordinate pretensions; under the name of genealogy, he demolished the concealed, diseased will to power of the inferiors, of the herd.

In order to realize *his* will to power, to claim a monopoly for *his* divine difference, Nietzsche had to unmask the resentment of others, and demystify society and human history as a whole. However, his self-transfiguration with an anthropological background was only half successful, that is to say, it was not successful, for the obvious reason that he applied his genealogy only to the desire of others and not to his own, since if he had applied it to himself it would have destroyed the whole enterprise. This illusory self-glorification, that did nothing but turn the most highly competitive imitation against the others in order to demonstrate Nietzsche's nonexistent independence from them, could only rebound ruinously to his detriment. He had to relaunch it but that necessitated utilizing yet again his denied imitative desire, his dependence on models, which was thus brought out painfully once more, and so on *ad infinitum*. In this way the entire system was tending towards explosion and collapse.

The more Nietzsche sought to divinize himself, the more he had to come to terms with his desire, but the more urgent and immediate the force of his desire became, the more irresistible the impulse to divinization. The more he tried to escape from the doubles crisis, the more these doubles multiplied under his eyes. Nietzsche could not, therefore, rest content with the exterior disguise of Dionysus, he had to gain possession of the god's innermost nature; as with Proteus, the essence of Dionysus is metamorphosis, the duplication of all possible masks. Nietzsche had need of a whole arsenal, a whole repertory of disguises. The single mask multiplied and became a series of masks. Dionysus became Zarathustra, and eventually ballooned to become a string of uncontrollably rotating, raving identities.

The first 'recurrence' to be 'eternal' in Nietzsche was the unresolved problem of his desire, his never-identified identity, defined in a letter to Overbeck as the "*wheel* of problems to which I am bound."[17] At the same time the eternal recurrence was the recurrence of ritual cycles, of sacrificial refoundations, of ancient mediations. The eternal recurrence was his hope of finding a new pagan (and in this sense neo-pagan) cycle, which only led to the eternal recurrence of cyclothymia, the exhausting swing from euphoria to depression, the typical result of an unresolved rivalry relationship. The "*wheel*" to which Nietzsche was chained like Prometheus became the self-feeding megalomania and coprophagy of his madness, the sacrificial circle that finally brought about his immolation. But the first circle, surely, is the circle of the persecutors, the circle that needs a center pin to whirl around and for all to strike, a center to surround and kill?

Towards the Center of the Labyrinth

The inflationary strategy adopted by Nietzsche to play with the Dionysian symbols brings out their structure, their anthropological origin. The evocatory power of the works of Nietzsche's maturity more than excuse the touches of *Biedermeier* found here and there in his early writings and is even more convincingly ferocious, as in the statement of intent contained in the following fragment:

> I love the splendid lack of restraint of a young predatory animal, that plays
> so prettily with its prey and, as it plays, tears it to pieces.[18]

The image is mystifying but at the same time it reveals the real nature of Nietzsche's 'game,' the hunt, in which Nietzsche identifies with the fascinating otherness of the unreachable predator that he would have to have been.

As previously with the tiger-like eyes attributed to Greek warriors, this is not simple animal violence contemplated in the misty vision of an aesthete, but concrete human violence in an animal disguise. In fact, both the panther and references to play are found among the symbols of Dionysus that represent the transformation within human culture of sacrificial rites into symbol. In Nietzsche's constant appeal to images from nature for the purpose of defending the cause of violence, with the idea that men must return to their 'naturalness,' he uses very ancient symbolism but in such an exaggerated, contrived, declamatory way that it becomes revealing, just like the eternal recurrence.[19] Human sacrifice, so often evoked in his writings, and defined as "the noble duty to sacrifice men" [*die hohe Pflicht, Menschen zu opfern*],[20] was anything but a simple continuation of the animal sphere: for Wagner's old rival it was his revenge on the whole world, along with his insane yet lucid desire to re-examine and give new meaning to the sacrificial foundations of antiquity.

This process, in which transfigured desire goes hand-in-hand with an enthralling, profound study in anthropology, can be observed in other fragments:

> The orgiastic soul
> I have seen: its eyes at least—they are eyes of honey,
> Now deep, calm, now green and lascivious
> His halcyon smile,
> The sky looked on bloody and cruel
>
> The orgiastic soul of woman
> I have seen, her halcyon smile, her eyes of honey, now deep and veiled, now
> green and lascivious, a trembling surface.
> Lascivious, somnolent, trembling, hesitant,
> The sea wells up in her eyes.[21]

Here we have not only the metamorphosis of Nietzsche's desire for Cosima-Arianna, which is evident from the next fragment in the Colli-Montinari edition,[22] but also a perception of the ancient ritual connection between erotism and sacrificial violence. In antiquity, the images of honey and blood became confused and are already found in Sumerian texts where sexual excitement takes on almost cannibalistic overtones. The text's nearly

symmetrical repetition is indicative of the symmetry reached in the final stage
of imitation. The rite that Nietzsche reconstructs and relives neurotically in
this fragment is the rite of hierogamy, the sacred marriage of Dionysus and
Arianna that is linked to Crete through the theme of the labyrinth. Originally the hierogamy must have ended in bloodshed, a hypothesis supported
by the myths of Arianna, abandoned or hanged on an island (a substitute
for the center of the labyrinth), and of the killing of the Minotaur, who is
Dionysus's double in taurine form.[23] The metaphor of the sea welling up in
another's eyes expresses the indifferentiation of the violent crisis that will
cause blood to flow from the victim, who is described as trembling and thus
supremely desirable; there is also an allusion here to the victim falling into
the hands not of a satanic partner, as yet, but of the community ready "as it
plays," to "tear it to pieces." The labyrinth is the perfect symbol of the doubles
crisis, of the circle closing in on a single preselected individual, while the sea
symbolizes the mob that there is no escape from, the sea in which Nietzsche
struggled desperately to save himself from drowning but, like Icarus, finally
sank beneath the waves. Icarus, who died by submersion in the sea, is a transformation of the victim submerged by the mob.

Nietzsche was not alone in mingling erotism with ritual violence. There
was growing awareness of anthropology in advanced European culture at
the time, leading to results that are worth examining briefly and comparing
to Nietzsche's achievements in this field. The preliminaries of Nietzsche's
sacrificial hierogamy become openly orgiastic in D'Annunzio's *The Flame of
Life*, in a scene describing Èffrena's desire for Foscarina, a "savage ardor" fired
by the public acclaim received a moment before as well as by the idea of an
erotic triangle just suggested to his mind by Foscarina herself:

> That turbid ardor came to him from far, far away, from the remotest ori-
> gins, from the primitive animality of sudden promiscuity, from the ancient
> mystery of sacred lusts. Like the god-possessed mob [*torma invasa dal dio*]
> descending the mountainside, uprooting trees and advancing in increas-
> ingly blind fury, its numbers swelling with more of the crazed, spreading
> madness everywhere in passing until it became a huge animal and human
> multitude moved by a monstrous will; and thus that raw instinct rushed

through him troubling and dragging with it all the figures of his spirit in its impetuous, infinite agitation. And what he most desired in the knowing, desperate woman [...] the passionate actress who passed from the frenzy of the crowd to the strength of the male, the Dionysian creature who crowned the mysterious rite with the act of life as in the Orgy. [...] He saw her in a flash, lying outstretched, full of the power that had drawn a howl from the monster, throbbing like a Maenad after the dance, thirsty and tired, but needing to be taken, to be shaken, to contract in a final spasm, to receive the violent seed, and grow calm at last in a dreamless drowse.—How many men had stepped out from the crowd to embrace her, having yearned for her lost in the unanimous mass [*massa unanime*]? Their desire had been made up of the desire of thousands, their vigor multifarious. Something of the drunkenness of the crowd [*popolo*], something of the fascinated monster, penetrated the fiber of the actress with the sensual pleasure [*voluttà*] of those nights.[24]

The collective aspect, that Nietzsche struggled to control, emerges imperiously in D'Annunzio. In *The Child of Pleasure* he is unequalled in his perception of what lies behind sexual pleasure, of the mimetic pressure of social models and the threatening presence of group desire, the desire of the masses. Erotism and Dionysian violence merge for the simple reason that they emanate from a single force, from mimetic mediation: it comes as no surprise, then, that they reinforce each another by turns, in a collective arousal where coupling amounts to rape and rape to ritual slaughter. The hyper-mimetic D'Annunzio is aware of the mass, 'breathes' it, in all that he says and, in contrast to Nietzsche's cerebral, unrealistic excesses, speaks with the concrete voice of experience. He tries to react to the Dionysian agitation that he perceives both inside and outside himself, by externalizing it in the form of dramatic gesture, in the public dimension of the stage. Only the Dionysus of drama can contain the Dionysus of the orgies. As Stelio Èffrena puts it to his friend, dreaming of an unprecedented tragic catharsis:

Have you ever seen the entire Universe appear before you, for a few seconds, looking like a human head? I have, a thousand times. Ah, to sever it with a single blow like Perseus when he cut off the head of the Medusa, and hold it up in front of the crowds from a scaffold so that they would never forget! Have you never thought that a great tragedy might resemble that gesture of Perseus?[25]

D'Annunzio dreams of an ultimate sacrifice to fulfill the unsatisfied desire that he senses in himself and in others, a sacrifice to be performed in public in all its stunning horror, that would enthrall and dominate the turbulent masses of contemporary Europe; and he also dreams of the new Wagnerian-D'Annunzian art of tragedy that should make it possible. However, rather than put a new sacrifice in place of the ancient representations, as in Nietzsche's scheme, D'Annunzio wanted to replace the ancient sacrifices with a new type of representation; their separate aims differed profoundly, though both were to prove illusory. Just like Nietzsche, Èffrena is fascinated and loses his way symbolically in the "primitive windings"[26] of the labyrinth, with Foscarina. She becomes the victim designate—Arianna—but Èffrena, unlike Nietzsche, eventually seeks the way out with her, showing that he still retains human ties. D'Annunzio always possessed a moral awareness and a playful, ironic tone that are not to be found in Nietzsche's monomaniacal, fanatical Dionysism.[27]

Nietzsche's orgiastic fragments and D'Annunzio's collective erotic orgy closely resemble the Dionysian nightmare in another work by a German writer, Thomas Mann's *Death in Venice*. At this point in the novella, the main character, Aschenbach, is obsessed by love for a boy and by fear of cholera, as it spreads through Venice progressing step by step with his desire. The final part of the dream shows us the innermost nature of Dionysus, the "stranger god," as he is defined by Mann, and by Euripides in *The Bacchae*:

> Great was his disgust, great his fear, and he sincerely wanted to hold firm to all that was his to the very end, against the stranger, the enemy of the steadfast, dignified spirit. But the din and the yelling re-echoed from the rocky walls, grew and multiplied, triumphantly swelling in an irresistible delirium. Vapors clouded his mind, the acrid smell of goats, the odor given off by panting bodies, and a stench like polluted water mixed with another familiar smell: of sores, of rife disease. The beating of the drums thundered in his heart, his head spun, blind fury seized him and intoxicating lust, and his soul yearned to join the Bacchanalia. The huge obscene wooden symbol was unveiled and raised aloft: and quivering more and more excitedly they

all shouted the ritual slogan. They foamed at the mouth in their agitation, spurred one other on with lewd gestures and lascivious hands, laughing and moaning; they pierced each other's flesh and licked the blood as it spurted out. And by now the dreamer was with them, in them, and subject to the stranger god. On the contrary, they were with him, when they threw themselves upon the animals, ripped them open and killed them, and swallowed the steaming mouthfuls of flesh; and when on the trampled ground they commenced horrific couplings in honor of the god. And his soul knew the taste of lust and the madness of perdition.[28]

A great admirer of Nietzsche the philosopher, whose inspiration is apparent here where Mann, like the true artist that he was, reveals what lay behind the "mortified sensibilities" of Aschenbach-Nietzsche. In an unforgettable description, we are shown the collective aspect of Dionysus, the aspect that hypnotized D'Annunzio but from which Nietzsche, otherwise so keen to extol the god, backed away. This was a far more terrible matter than the trauma suffered by the innocent youth in Mann's reconstruction; this was the repressed 'trauma' of an entire age, of an entire civilization. With his pathetically "steadfast, dignified spirit," Aschenbach plunges headlong into the orgy and so symbolizes Europe driven by its uncontrolled rivalries and hiding behind a militaristic ideology, as illustrated by Nietzsche himself as a young man, and soon to charge like a wild bull into the wholesale slaughter of the First World War. We should not be taken in by the otherness of the "stranger god," because what is being shown to us is an otherness inherent in ourselves at a more primitive, deeper level of personal identity. The unbridled sexual license of the rite is a means not an end in itself: the real object of desire is to gorge on "steaming mouthfuls of flesh" in the paroxysm of the *sparagmós*, the homophagy, what Euripides calls "homophagic joy," that is, the joy of devouring still-living flesh.[29] Originally, there were human victims instead of animals, there was Dionysus himself. The erotic orgies were basically a prelude, the inertial track leading to the supreme transgression, the savage killing that was ritually repeated to prevent it occurring within the group. By means of these rites ancient Greece sought to defend itself from the massacre of mimetic violence, something that modern Europe could no longer do. In Mann's *The Magic Mountain*, the principle character, Hans Castorp, has a similar dream that completes and glosses Aschenbach's dream, and shows the revenge taken by D'Annunzio's Tullio Hermil in a real 'genealogical' key: the dream is set in the paradise of Hellas, home to the "children of the Sun," as Castorp calls them, and the victim devoured raw is a small child, as in the Orphic myth of the child Dionysus eaten alive by the Titans.[30] Avant-garde Western art of the period began to pullulate with sacrificial visions of this kind. On the eve of the First World War, the savage dance rhythms of man's origin, culminating in human sacrifice, were heard again in the subterranean sounds of Stravinsky's *Le Sacre du printemps* [*The Rite of Spring*].

Nietzsche's daring exploration made it possible for Mann to depict the scene in *Death in Venice* so magnificently but its explicit character, and moral awareness, are unlike anything to be found in the philosopher of the will to power: in Nietzsche Dionysian violence is synonymous of good health but in *Death in Venice* it is a symptom of degradation and disease. Not even Mann was willing to draw the ultimate conclusions from the anthropological truths that had begun to emerge with Nietzsche. Like D'Annunzio, but in a less Mediterranean and less ostentatious manner, he gave with one hand what he took away with the other, revealing and at the same time concealing the truth, filtering it in two ways, first, through the socially-recognized and prestigious mask of literary invention and, second, through the form of the oneiric vision which, from a psychological viewpoint, attenuated the horror of the epiphany. The very inhumanity of Nietzsche's statements of principle reveal the mimetic intensity of his experience; and Mann drew on this for his own anthropological and psychological investigations, with his moral aware-ness and skill both enhanced as a result of Nietzsche's recklessness. In his pathologically impulsive manner, Nietzsche dug out the material that Mann wove into the magical, ironical webs of his art, trying to regain the control that had been dangerously lost.

With ambiguity worthy of Goethe Mann intended to protect himself from the risks that Nietzsche was prepared to run as a matter of course in order to scrutinize the dim mimetic depths. The author of *Death in Venice*, sensing vaguely that the mimetico-mythological machinery set in motion by Nietzsche was a deadly trap from which he had not come out alive, preferred to make the artistic doubles of his own creating die in place of himself. Both Mann and D'Annunzio made use of literary objectification in this way; Nietzsche, on the contrary, never succeeded in utilizing this resource and only briefly touched on it in an early fragment, *Euphorion*. He was forced to relive in his own person the doubles that he refused to recognize, to the point where he reproduced the collective mimeticism that he had exorcized, and multiplied everyone's desire within himself: in his last letter to Burckhardt he declared himself to be "every name in history."[31] The urge to flee from himself and from others resulting from his dissociation brought this Dionysian actor into a wasteland, to an empty stage where he relived the doubles of his life, and therefore of every life. No elegant loophole, no literary objectification could save him from this bitterly theatrical fate, this stage performance, instructive for others but not for himself.

What is most eloquent about Nietzsche's transfigurations of the myth of the labyrinth is the absolute otherness of his desire, personified for him by Cosima and Richard Wagner and, since this is the same otherness as the otherness of mythology and the archaic sacred, mythicized introspection becomes introspection of myth. Just as Nietzsche's references to myths must not be taken literally, so they must not be seen as only a disguise. Dionysus and Arianna certainly are disguises but this is because they present us with the originary, ancestral disguise of the man killed to become a god. This anthropological archeology interacted in a deadly fashion with the frustrations that fuelled it. Nietzsche wanted to assimilate to Dionysus and Arianna, to take their place, but since this divine desire arose from imitative dependence on others, and therefore from his experience of *not* being god, to identify with the god amounted to experimental proof of failure. However, the god who failed refused to give up the fight, and reacted in the only way conceivable for him, that is, by living in his own person what is objectified and described in Aschenbach's nightmare and the wild vision of Stelio Èffrena. The glorifier of Dionysus wanted not simply to put on the mask of the god but to *become* the mask. That, however, would have meant transforming himself into the simulacrum of the killed victim, leaving himself open to scrutiny by the mass, the crowd that he despised yet secretly courted, it meant casting himself into the undifferentiated sea of insanity.

> Nothing like it has ever been written in a poem, never experienced, never suffered: a god suffers thus, a Dionysus. [. . .] Who, apart from myself, knows what Arianna is! . . .[32]

Even while concealing the truth of his desire, Nietzsche became the heroic seismograph, the 'historian' recording this concealment, so sensitive as to become its revelation; and since the concealment that defined him is the same as the concealment of man's entire sacrificial history, Nietzsche and his destiny were transformed and became a recapitulation of that history.[33] Unable to reclose the 'pit' of his sacrificial foundation, he went on digging till he buried himself, as an image recurrent in his writings suggests, the image of the lair or cave,[34] Zarathustra's cave, the cave into which Nietzsche wanted to crawl in order to sleep.[35] The cave is another archaic place of sacrifice, another ancient version of the labyrinth, and clearly it was to prove less and less able to supply the hoped-for salvation: increasingly the deep recesses underground sent Nietzsche back to the dark and unaccepted sides of his psyche, to the insanity awaiting him,[36] to bring him ironic fame that no sane person would envy.

Disastrous Divinization and Mass Extermination

In *Beyond Good and Evil* Nietzsche describes the "manifold martyrdom" of a psychologist and "soul diviner" who examines the inner ruin and the deceptions concealed behind "great men" but, where everyone else feels "great veneration," he learns to feel "great pity along with great scorn," which leads him to ask this revealing question:

> And who knows if exactly the same thing has not happened with all great events up till now: the multitude has worshipped a god—and the "god" has been only a poor sacrificial victim![37]

This striking passage, that quite rightly impressed such commentators as Lou Salomé and De Lubac,[38] is a direct development of the assertion about the violent death of God; this time, though, the madman's projection, with its impossible daydream of an unprecedented sacrificial foundation, breaks up in a kaleidoscope of sacrificial elements: Nietzsche is the martyred diviner of souls, the scrutinizer of great men's intestines, and himself one of these great men. The disgust of Nietzsche the haruspex was aroused by what he spasmodically wanted to become, by what he felt he would become. Great men are poor sacrificial victims in the sense that everyone imitates their desire to incarnate the 'mythic' difference to be venerated but, for this incarnation to happen, the community applies the ancestral transference of the divinized victim postmortem, necessarily in a transformed and trivialized fashion. The great modern man, 'idolized' by the public, deluded himself in thinking that he could become a god with impunity, and incautiously evoked a collective illusion that operates in the only way known to it, as a concealing tombstone under whose weight the victim, finally famous, is buried, dead or alive as the case may be. The famous personality was a failure because he saw a reflection of his own desire, multiplied a thousandfold and transformed into a lethal trap, in the multitude who tore him to pieces and adored him. For the psychologist in Nietzsche, the nature of the whole business, atrocious and cheap, was sheer torture because it was a reminder of his dependence and a foretaste of his future mortal sufferings; it made plain to him the real nature of his ontological ambition, the ever-open wound of envy and resentment. Great men—he adds below—show themselves to have "souls accustomed to hide any cracks," they show themselves to be

> men who often take revenge through their works for something foul within themselves, who often, in their outbursts, seek to consign a too-faithful memory to oblivion, who are often lost in the mire and almost love it, coming to resemble will-o'-the-wisps wandering over the marshes and *pretending* to be stars . . .[39]

It is not hard to recognize "something foul within" as the rivalry with Wagner and the "too-faithful memory" as the obsessive memory of Wagner, stronger than ever now that the *Pater Seraphicus* was dead. The recurrent image of the star now reveals its bogus, mortuary nature. Nietzsche is the prophetic ghost (the "clown") of the fame that he had long invoked, the funereal commentator on his own posthumous identity, which he described in *The Gay Science*, after evoking the masks and spectral appearances used as a defense against others:

> . . . would we be content to burden ourselves with this isolation, this coldness, this deathly silence, all this underground solitude, hidden, dumb and inviolate, that we call life but might well be called death, if we did not know what *will become* of us—and know that only after death will

we posthumous men attain to *our* life and come alive, ah! so very much alive?[40]

He tried in vain to exorcise the contorted, indirect admission of the truth by putting it in the form of a question and using the first person plural (the speaker is one of the posthumous men). Nietzsche continued to formulate the enigma of his own fate with no wish to resolve it, waiting for it to 'resolve' him. Already in *Human, All Too Human* the dilemma of the chase, to devour or be devoured, an exciting dilemma in its way, manifested itself as a paralyzing choice between being devoured by others or devouring oneself in the "underground solitude, hidden, dumb and inviolate," the cave-tomb refuge of last resort:

> *From the country of the cannibals.* In solitude the solitary man devours himself, among the multitude he is devoured by many. Take your choice.[41]

What first strikes us here is not the romantic, tragic isolation of the solitary man but the fact that cannibalism is as much an attribute of the solitary man as of the "many." This illusory difference of the solipsistic hero goes straight back to the indifferentiation of the doubles of violence, to the savage indistinctness of human origin. The solitary man's desire is no less primitive and savage than the craving of the others. What is really dramatic for him is that he has no way out of the violent doubles through the unconscious sacrifice of another person. The dilemma underlines both an awareness of sacrifice and a refusal to recognize any other logic than sacrifice.[42] This implies that violence would multiply and strike the promoter of violence. In the impotent rage of his frustrated desire, Nietzsche theorized this escalation, and came to hope that all mankind might share his fate. At this point some alarming scenarios open up before us.

The impossibility of real sacrificial catharsis, of one last, definitive, bloody reprisal stretched the chain of violent imitations to infinity, broadened the duel-suicide to include all mankind, and transformed the dream of sacrificial palingenesis into a mass self-sacrifice. As *Daybreak* puts it:

> *A tragic epilogue to knowledge.* Of all the means for elevation, human sacrifice has done most in every age to stimulate and raise mankind. And perhaps any

other aspiration could always be ousted by a *single* huge thought, that might bring victory to smile on the most victorious,—by the thought, that is, of *a self-sacrificing mankind*. But to whom should it sacrifice itself?[43]

The endless competitive-sacrificial chain that represents Nietzsche's universe of doubles could never attain its goal which was the divine difference whose major, most stimulating source in the past had been human sacrifice. It would be necessary therefore to find the *ultimate* human sacrifice, the sacrifice capable of interrupting the doubles and snatching victory from the "most victorious," but modern sacrifice no longer works and, in the hope of making it work, would have to be repeated *ad nauseam*, as Girard holds, or rather to be performed in an extraordinary and 'definitive' fashion, till it coincides in either case with the destruction of the entire chain of doubles, with the self-destruction of mankind as a whole.[44] In other words, sacrifice explodes, degenerates, becomes insane. To what monstrous divinity should this impossible 'rite' be dedicated? This would fulfill the cult of the madman in *The Gay Science*, according to whom we must ourselves "become gods," that is, a human race of 'madmen' in which, clearly, if all become gods it is because all become dead. Nietzsche's contradictory knowledge could have only this "tragic epilogue." The rest of the aphorism from *Daybreak* makes this epilogue tragic and at the same time grotesque, when the philosopher imagines mankind offering itself in a holocaust to the inhabitants of other planets. Science fiction would appear to be the last refuge of the failed neo-foundation but Nietzsche's sinister greatness lies in his prophetic anticipation of the absurd, revealing situation of mankind today.[45]

This conclusion shows us the real face of Nietzsche's nihilism, a petrifying Medusa's face. Foreseen by the philosopher of the will to power as a necessary preparatory phase for the achievement of his ideas, this "ecstatic nihilism" was capable of going beyond all that was "too human,"[46] a nihilism in which supreme knowledge coincided with the destruction of those who knew.

This fatal 'ecstasy' reappeared in a fragment written in 1888 where the tone was even more frenzied as that final moment approached:

... we teach philosophy as a concept *that can cost one's life*: how could we be of greater help in this? For mankind, the value of a concept will always be what it costs mankind. If nobody hesitates to sacrifice thousands of lives for the concepts of "God," "fatherland" and "freedom," and if history is a great smoke screen for this kind of sacrifice, how can we demonstrate the *excellence* of the concept of "philosophy" over and above popular values such as "God," "fatherland" and "freedom" if not by the fact that it costs *more*, it costs *greater* numbers of lives? . . . Transvaluation of all values: *it will be very costly*, let me tell you—[47]

Nietzsche's youthful vision of Olympus, from which he wanted to exclude a growing mass of slaves, and his complacency as a "*merry*" bystander during the Nice earthquake find their final expression here. This hecatomb, this mass self-destruction is the final outcome of his sacrificial game, and there can be no doubt that if mankind unconsciously followed the advice of the philosopher of the will to power, it would mark its most ironic and macabre triumph, or rather, it would be its most macabre and ironic refutation. Starting with the First World War, the philosophy of the hecatomb was enthusiastically applied throughout the century which has just ended, and we wonder inevitably, not without a measure of apprehension, what the present century holds in store for us. Will there be an after-mankind in the wake of mass terrorism, of a nuclear or ecological holocaust?[48]

The Final Enemy

These warnings should be cause for reflection in anyone who is willing to give words and thoughts the value that they really deserve. However, in the face of Nietzsche's 'self-fulfilling' nihilism, the moment has come when we should go back to a question that we have not tackled directly as yet: how was it that Nietzsche could move with this unchecked freedom, play so riskily with a foundation that ought to remain hidden, and amuse himself so tragically with forces on whose control the survival of mankind depends? Perhaps it is worth repeating that the Greeks, who were certainly no pacifists, never dreamt even just to think of such things. What Greek would have dared to assert that human sacrifices had always been the most noble and stimulating "means of elevation"? As Karl Löwith observes, referring to the eternal recurrence and the will to power: "All this superlative, 'supreme' and 'extreme' willing and unwilling, creating and transforming, is as anti-natural as it is non-Greek," and again: "While men in antiquity preserved their means with a sense of measure since they were naturally violent, modern man tends towards the extreme [*zum Extrem*]—in order not to be mediocre."[49] Löwith himself fails to grasp the full significance of these penetrating remarks, and the extent to which they interact with the conscious and half-conscious strategies adopted by Nietzsche.[50] What would this modern man with his pathological tendency "towards the extreme" not be capable of doing in order "not to be mediocre"?[51]

Even when the Greeks attained a partial revelation of the nature of Dionysus, as in the case of Euripides, they were very careful not to identify with him, indeed they took fright and backed away, like Agave at the end of *The Bacchae*, having torn her son Pentheus to pieces in the Dionysian madness. As Nietzsche secretly knows but refuses to admit openly, the reason why he can talk about Dionysus with a reckless freedom and mad audacity that is anything but Greek is because he belongs to a society influenced by a religion that demystifies all violence, renders it visible, and offers a completely different alternative; and because he lives in a world conditioned, much against its will, by a religion that persists in silently showing the collective murder of God to disbelieving humanity.

Christianity alone supplied Nietzsche with the awareness of the victim that emerges from his writings with such intensity, matched by the efforts he made to forget it, to transfigure it by pretending that it was 'natural,' and claim it for his own by deceit. It is awareness of the victim that makes more acceptable and human the image of Nietzsche conveyed through his writings. How regrettable, though, that this solitary philosopher was not guilty of the *felix culpa* of being more often, and more humanly, inconsistent! In *The Gay Science*, for example, he could describe to perfection the fate of the victims and the stifling of their voices in the persecutory unconscious:

> *Sacrifice.* As to sacrifice and the spirit of sacrifice, victims take a different view from spectators: but from time immemorial they have never been given a chance to express it.[52]

And in *Daybreak* he had already written with striking concision:

Bear this in mind! The person punished is no longer the person who did
the deed. He is always a scapegoat.[53]

The definition has a geometrical brevity and precision. The person
who is guilty or presumed guilty is punished, at the most primitive level,
not because any responsibility has been ascertained but because someone
has to pay for the ills suffered by the community by taking them on himself,
permitting the community *anyhow* to vent its desire for revenge that would
otherwise multiply crazily. A scapegoat, therefore.

It is precisely this lucidity that brings us to the crux of the matter, the
contradiction at the heart of Nietzsche's system of doubles and his attempt
to use it as a completely novel means of self-divinization. To state so radically,
as Nietzsche states, that God is dead was only possible in a world aware of the
death of Christ, the son of God who died so that nobody became god after he
was killed, so that nobody should be killed anymore. And in a world where
violence can no longer follow the route of sacrifice and remorseless killing of
rivals, the doubles of violence inevitably tend to multiply not only in society
but also within the individual. Mental disorders now take the place of
the doubles' states of possession that once led to sacrifice. This is the reason
why Nietzsche yearned for the Dionysian *mania*, so effectively exemplified
in Èffrena's vision and Aschenbach's dream. By means of the new meaning
given to the ancient madness the philosopher hoped to liberate himself from
the modern madness afflicting him but the outcome, as we have seen, was
paralyzing and destructive.

Rejection of Christ was therefore inevitable, fated to happen right from
the start, from his earliest writings; accompanying his evolution as a thinker,
it came to torment him more and more.[54] He refused to recognize that, if
Christianity makes it easier for the doubles to multiply within the individual
and within society, it is solely because Christianity makes human violence
visible but leaves every decision to the individual human being. He can
choose his own violence, and that way leads to madness, or he can choose
the concrete alternative of *conversion*, that is, 'turn' to look into himself, recognize his own violence and accept the message that demystifies it. This is so
far true that Christianity's active part in history can be described as a gradual
demolition of all the intermediate alternatives between, on the one hand,

individual and collective madness and, on the other, the "kingdom of God," of love prevailing without violence.[55]

Christianity therefore represents everything that Nietzsche rejected, everything from which he had to defend himself at all costs. His resentment reached its apogee when confronted by what was for him the archetype of 'herd morality': Christianity's sickening defense of the weak, of the unsuccessful that Nietzsche, at his most darkly sanguine, would reduce to pulp or transform into cannon fodder for the advantage of the 'strongest,' the Olympus of the aristocratic, the supermen, with the exponential dynamic that leads to mass extermination.

If we are to understand Nietzsche's ruthless attitude towards the weak and, above all, towards Christianity, defender of the weak, we need to remember its nature as a tactic of substitution tied in with a repressed awareness of his role as victim, as defeated rival. Sacrifice is always substitution, it means having someone else die in place of ourselves, in place of everyone: if the mechanism fails to work, then the life of everyone is set at risk. And substitution can momentarily save the victim: this happens when, in the chaos surrounding the instant when the victim is chosen and killed, he is not immediately killed but another individual is killed instead; the original victim is allowed to live, not as a god who has died and is reborn but as a living god, as a priest-king, to be sacrificed as soon as his powers are seen to be no longer effective.[56] Every victim saved by Christianity was, then, one victim fewer for the sacrificial machine intended to guarantee Nietzsche's power and survival. These victims were to die *instead of* Nietzsche. He behaved like an ancient priest-king, but with a superior consciousness, who had to make the sacrificial laws of the community his own, and whose life might be said to be safe only as long as he fulfilled this role of safeguarding and administering the laws, and found 'raw material' to sacrifice in his place. By jamming the substitution mechanism on which this philosopher-king based his precarious existence, Christianity, the religion of the weak, with its debilitating effect on "the strength, responsibility and noble duty to sacrifice men,"[57] threatened his life. The famous transvaluation of all values was a program to confute and reject all Christian values in view of this objective, which also enables us to see why it was to enjoy subsequent public success. All of us, surely, in our less remarkable ways, feel the need for substitution? Here more than anywhere else Nietzsche proved to be the vanguard of a rebellion destined to become a mass phenomenon. If Christ was intent on removing the mask of Nietzsche-Dionysus, then the latter had to show that the real mask to demystify, the real lie, the false idol to be toppled, was Christ. It was a life-and-death struggle, the development and completion of the duel with Wagner. Christ was the real white whale that Nietzsche-Ahab sought to hunt to the death through the seas of human origin, tragically followed by the crew of the Pequod, by the masses and their leaders in Germany, in Europe, and in the world.[58]

Nietzsche's transition from rivalry with Wagner to rivalry with Christ is documented in a letter to Malwida von Meysenbug written in April 1883 where his identification with the antichrist bursts from the page, under the effect of Wagner's death and Cosima's icy silence: "Do you want a name to call me by? The language of the Church has one: I am——the *Antichrist*."[59] This is the first clear signal of Nietzsche's final battle to settle accounts with all those who had humbled, mocked, or excluded him. Convinced of his genealogy, he was certain that by incarnating the part of their enemy he could demystify, once and for all, the hypocrisy of the Christians, the 'virtuous,' the 'herd.' Like a poker player when the stakes are raised, after lasting for nearly two thousand years, he decided to go and *see*.

So, in the spring of 1888, Nietzsche came to discover something that had never been so clearly understood before: the difference between Dionysus and Christ, something that neither D'Annunzio nor Thomas Mann managed to identify and articulate, and so great a discovery that it has passed unobserved. Not even commentators such as Löwith, who were so perspicacious in diagnosing Nietzsche's contradictions, had an inkling of the Christian 'secret' that this lone navigator had managed to extract: any recognition of the sort on their part would have forced them to admit that Nietzsche's investigations were not grounded in a more predictable philosophy but in anthropology and religion (i.e., in my terms, in a new type of philosophy). The better Christian interpreters of Nietzsche, such as De Lubac, have suffered similar blindness but with a difference: in their case the foundation that Nietzsche fought is fully present and accepted. Girard has been the only interpreter to do justice to Nietzsche on this point. His interpretation of Nietzsche has life because his ideas enable us to make a living study of how the Christian message works in depth, even though this goes beyond Girard's formulation.

Unlike the anthropologists of his own day and the mass of cultural relativists of ours, Nietzsche grasped the fact that the structural equality of events concerning Dionysus and Christ was not proof of their identity but of their profound difference. Both are killed but while the story of Dionysus is told from the standpoint of the persecutors, who see Dionysus as inciting them to sacrifice, the story of Christ's Crucifixion and Resurrection makes us see that the violence is done by the mob, the victim being completely innocent. Once again, however, Nietzsche's marvelous intuition stopped short: just as he failed to openly recognize the role of the mob in Dionysus, which makes a significant but fleeting appearance in the fragment about Dionysus versus Christ Crucified, so the aspiring antichrist was also unwilling to see that if Christ remained the innocent victim right to the end it was because he remained completely immune to the imitative contagion of his persecutors. The frightening strength of the contagion can be seen in Greek tragedy, for example in Euripides, when Dionysus lures Pentheus to follow him to a horrific death on Mount Cithaeron. In other words, Nietzsche refused to really recognize Christ's innocence, unwilling and unable to admit that He was completely untouched by the infernal farrago described in *The Bacchae*, while his own infernal rancor was part of it. In the Gospels this total innocence in Jesus is the concrete demonstration, invisible to those unwilling to see it, that He is the son of God; this power transcending the doubles of human violence enables him to forgive that violence already from the cross and makes his Resurrection not the return of the divinized victim but the revelation of the indestructible, living victim, whose divinity does not depend on the violent transfiguration of the persecutors because it reveals it, bears the signs of it and demystifies it,[60] without any accusation or act of revenge.[61] Christ has nothing to do with duelling, with the mimetic rivalry game, in whose terms Nietzsche compelled himself to think.

Nietzsche had to defend himself from this truth that threatened to undermine the doubles game that both sustained him and held him captive. In his eyes, the difference between Dionysus and Christ could only show that the truth lay with Dionysus, and that the difference had to become Dionysus's battle against the crucified Christ. The provocative, fanatical identification declared to Malwida von Meysenbug became the solitary, unseemly challenge of *The Antichrist*, the final attack that marked his definitive mental breakdown. Refusal of the only alternative to the closed universe of the doubles ensured their triumph in his tottering mental state, the triumph of insanity.

Girard has called Nietzsche the greatest religious thinker of the nineteenth century, presenting the aphorism about Dionysus versus the crucified Christ as the greatest theological text of the nineteenth century.[62] Both definitions may appear to be exaggerated if we think, for example, of the religious truths discovered by Alessandro Manzoni, who based his conception on a different awareness of Christianity and of the mechanisms governing the mob and desire. As a young man Nietzsche admired Manzoni's masterpiece *I promessi sposi* [*The Betrothed*]; at least, he said so, though the results are not apparent.[63] Girard, however, was not thinking about what Nietzsche actually produced, so much as what he came across by chance as his whaler ploughed through far northern seas. In that sense he was a genuine explorer of *terra incognita*, the greatest religious *discoverer* of the nineteenth century, but he was nevertheless an inverted discoverer, whose denials throw light on what he discovered and denied. A light-bringing denier, literally a *Lucifer*.[64]

CHAPTER 5

The Antichrist and the Crucifixion

An Infernal Initiation

In the last few months of his conscious existence, the opposition of Dionysus to Christ did not bring Nietzsche the solace that he had expected; on the contrary, it was a source of ever-increasing irritation and led him to make further futile efforts at destruction. Driven by his growing resentment, the doubles crisis that defined the mask of Zarathustra began to oscillate wildly and started to destroy the simulacrum that should have hidden it. Seized by mounting fury, Nietzsche redoubled his writings and projects hoping to bring about a definitive confrontation. Having completed *The Case of Wagner*, he set aside the projected *Will to Power* and *Transvaluation of All Values*[1] and concentrated his efforts on one last attempt at destruction, this time total and direct. With this work, *The Antichrist*, Nietzsche the hunter made his final move, his last bid to win the game, the real *Transvaluation of All Values* as the book was originally subtitled, that is, the "curse of Christianity" as the definitive subtitle, changed at the last minute,[2] made clear, by which it meant, to be exact, the curse destined to destroy Christianity.

A singular work among so many singular works by the same author, singular for the crazy and yet clear-sighted strategy that steers it, and for the systematic absence of any real inquiry into the contents resulting from that strategy. *The Antichrist* proposes a destructive, sinister complicity that sets the head spinning, so sinister that Girard himself prefers to avoid direct confrontation; it is like a narcotic intended to lead at long last to the sacrificial rite, with Christianity as the *right* victim, the truly guilty victim that it is just and liberating to slaughter and tear to pieces. The reader is invited to connive at this dark and contagious complicity, and he must show the toughest strands of his moral fiber if he is to react against it. *The Antichrist* is an initiation trial, whose survivors alone can learn Nietzsche's ultimate secrets and, in a negative form, the ultimate secrets of Christianity. No wonder that believers and nonbelievers alike give it a wide berth. Nonbelievers, in the majority as usual, take Nietzsche's efforts at their face value and mistake his propaganda for victory, seeing his apotheosis in what is almost a textbook demonstration of revelatory defeat.[3] *The Antichrist* is a description of Nietzsche's hell, a crazy and brilliant formulation of the infernal underground of the modern world. Like Dante in *The Divine Comedy*, we, too, must descend and pass through that hell in order to escape it. The journey will be shorter and less fascinating than Dante's but nonetheless full of unexpected incidents and dreadful revelations.

A detailed analysis of some key passages in *The Antichrist*, which Verrecchia describes as "vigorous" and "one of the most daring attacks on Christianity ever made,"[4] will suffice for us to grasp the real nature of the final battle waged by Nietzsche. Verrecchia has not the least suspicion of what Nietzsche was trying to do here, no idea that his attack was daring precisely because it was anything but 'vigorous' in the sense that he intends. The real problems remain luminously invisible. Verrecchia, who perceptively defines *The Antichrist* "as the work of a theologian turned upside down," is unaware of how exactly his definition hits the mark and confines his comments to noting that the celebrated phrase "'God is dead' is just a quip and means nothing in philosophy or sociology";[5] this is another observation that carries far more truth than its author intended since neither academic philosophy nor the social sciences have paid any attention to the literal meaning of Nietzsche's aphorism. Another leading interpreter of Nietzsche, Giorgio Colli, in his introduction to *The Antichrist*, provides instead a good example of the blindness that exists about the book. Colli wonders what sense there was in Nietzsche's attack, since "in those days the Christian doctrine was already more laughable than formidable."[6] He repeats this opinion elsewhere:

> As a physician of civilization, Nietzsche is above all an excellent diagnostician, with a prophetic streak. What he prophesied was to come true, and only too soon. As a religion, Christianity is just a relic these days, and the animosity towards it has died down as well . . .[7]

Christianity is so far a relic, and Nietzsche's prophecy has come true so soon, that the secret of *The Antichrist*, the secret of his disastrous defeat, has yet to be revealed. There is so little truth in the assertion of a decline in animosity towards Christianity, that expulsion from Christianity has been made a prerequisite, as far as much of contemporary culture is concerned, for anyone who wants to be numbered among the free spirits, to be considered aware and socially presentable; unless, that is, we recognize this diminished animosity in the icy silence that disdains to consider Christian arguments. The irony is that all this is said and done in the name of cultural values. At this point we might really start to wonder, if Nietzsche was "a physician of civilization," what civilization are we talking about. But now let us see how far his followers could trust the anti-Christian answers given by this "excellent diagnostician."

With far greater insight and courage than many of those who adopted his ideas, Nietzsche tried to do what they then assumed had been done, while they carefully avoided checking to see whether the statements had any basis in fact. *The Antichrist* appears as a kind of battle flag, condensing the scheme of all the anti-Christian criticisms made by modern culture, for which Nietzsche provides a convenient mask; and it appears no accident that a scholar with expert knowledge of the philosopher, such as Colli, regards the matter as closed independently of Nietzsche. It is best not to look too closely at the mask. With the systematic blindness of those who do not want to see, modern anti-Christianity refuses to recognize its own violence, and the fact that Christianity insists on talking about violence as freely chosen by men is taken as a sure sign that Christianity is itself violent, is indeed the source of violence. Besides, this line of argument must prove fatal. To accuse Christians of making victims, and then make Christianity the *ultimate victim*, can only demonstrate the truth of Christianity's underlying assumptions, a truth whose real nature is only the more evident when it is Christians themselves that violate it, since they are the ones who ought to bear witness to it. This logical observation on historical fact might be taken as the authentic prophecy for our age, exposing the true nature of those other prophecies that are to "come true and only too soon" in Colli's words. The entire *Antichrist* is an inverted prophecy; turned upside down it is the truth, the truth that Nietzsche, the "upside down theologian," rejected and finally, in an insane way, came to incarnate.

In *The Antichrist* Christianity is identified with the labyrinth, to which Nietzsche said he was predestined: he promises "a way out from thousands of years of the labyrinth," that is, from the doubles crisis, for which, according to him, the Christians are entirely to blame. But if Christianity is the labyrinth, then Christ is its center. The philosopher Theseus appears recalcitrant in the face of this center, and performs various diversionary maneuvers that are extremely instructive to reconstruct. For several chapters he tries to divide the enemy forces in order to hit them harder, reviving the old argument that makes a distinction between the figure of Christ and the historical development of Christianity. The logic of the doubles, if applied to Christianity, inevitably duplicates and divides it. This part of *The Antichrist* contains some evocative intuitions, owing to the use of Tolstoy as well:[8] Christ's distancing himself from all sacral religions, his preaching a new freedom to be achieved here and now in a life lived to the full and not ransomed to violence.[9] For a moment Nietzsche almost seems to recognize in this his claim about the 'innocence of becoming,' his polemic against the hypocritical condemnation of the real world in the name of other unreal worlds, in actual fact, is charged with more or less mystified violence. Did Nietzsche, now on the verge of mental breakdown, suspect how much this polemic was indebted to Christianity for what was authentic in it? This is a fair question, and a necessary one, not so much for what Nietzsche may have thought subjectively as for the objective reality that he touched on. It is this reality that asks the question, asking it of the text constantly. Nietzsche took the right direction for this question to be asked more and more forcibly by the things that he wrote and did. At the same time, the very possibility horrified him and he refused to believe it, resorting to all readily available means in an attempt to silence it once and for all. He drove himself towards the original source from which the message sprang, hoping to shut it off, to dry it up forever. But he was finally overwhelmed and met his fate there.

Christ Insulted

The self-destructive nature of the collision course followed by Nietzsche can be gauged by the verbal abuse and blasphemy employed, giving the lie in the most direct way to the romantic idea that Nietzsche abstained from attacking Christ.[10] The principle and blasphemous insult, repeated in *The Antichrist*, is that Christ was an idiot. This is even more plainly stated in several of the last fragments, as in this particularly brutal fragment:

> The "Jesus" type
> Jesus is *the very opposite of a genius* [das *Gegenstück eines Genies*]: he is an *idiot* [*Idiot*].[11]

The psychiatric classification becomes a harsh rhetorical question in another passage:

> . . . But can you be more grossly mistaken than when you make a genius [*Genie*] of Christ, who was an idiot [*Idiot*]?[12]

In this late fragment and in the corresponding passage in *The Antichrist*, the references to Dostoevsky's *Idiot* are explicit[13] but in no way contradict the use of the term as an insult, given that the novel's hero, Prince Myshkin, represents a degraded and ineffectual type of redeemer, an idealistic and impotent imitation of Christ.[14] Astutely simplifying for his own convenience, Nietzsche took Dostoevsky's ruthless analysis as the correct interpretation of Christ; in that way the abusive epithet retained its most obvious, precise meaning.[15] A further insult offered by Nietzsche is 'ass,' which he picked up from pagan accusations claiming that the Christians worshipped a god with an ass's head.[16] The intention to offend is no less evident than the skillful way in which historical and cultural references are stratified on several levels. Nietzsche applied the epithet of 'idiot' to Parsifal, the 'pure madman' hero of the opera that was Wagner's homage to Christ, the opera that Nietzsche hated and admired more than any other. The almost theological mediation through the model of Wagner makes still more evident, were it needed, Nietzsche's will to destroy the founder of Christianity by abuse and, transitively, to destroy all those who turned to Christ. One blasphemous remark sums up all the rest: "The idiot on the cross . . . [*Der Idiot am Kreuze*]."[17] The state of mental degradation attributed to Christ is the same into which Nietzsche himself is about to fall,[18] but the coarseness and vulgarity of his blasphemous projection must not close our eyes to its anthropological significance.

Profanity is an inverted prayer, holding God responsible for mankind's ills; it concisely expresses men's violent idea of god, formed for the archaic reason that their ancient gods were only men killed and divinized. Man blasphemes against God because he would like him killed in place of himself, which would be to perform the most ancient of sacrificial substitutions: this is the actual definition of mankind's original guilt, the significance of Adam and Eve's disobedience disclosed most brutally. The first parents of mankind cursed God because they interpreted him as an enemy, a rival, as an envious divinity whom they in turn came to envy. But the envy, the rivalry that became violence, was theirs alone. In his eagerness to rebel theologically, a sentiment shared by most people in the modern world, Nietzsche could hardly fail to touch on this point as well; in chapter 48 he tells the story of the original sin from the only viewpoint that he believed could, and should, be valid, *the serpent's viewpoint*, that is, from the viewpoint of what the Christian tradition defines as Satan. Girard shows us how Satan corresponds to the violent image that men have always formed of the gods and God, and personifies the violent logic of the doubles.

Already, in 1882, at the time of writing *The Gay Science*, in a fragment whose typographical stresses produce revealing and almost uncontrollable emphases, Nietzsche declared:

> I have experienced, voluntarily and thoroughly, the OPPOSITE to a RELIGIOUS NATURE. I know the *devil* and the *perspectives from which* HE *looks towards God.*[19]

Just as nobody has taken the aphorism about the death of God literally, so nobody has understood how seriously these words were to be taken. The future antichrist, soon to declare his identity to Malwida von Meysenbug, had come to know the devil thoroughly and fully understood his point of view.

A shadow hung over Nietzsche from his earliest writings, a specter that can only be defined as demoniacal:

> What I fear is not the horrifying figure behind my chair, but its voice; and not the words, but the terribly inarticulate and inhuman tone of this figure. If only it spoke as men speak![20]

The most disturbing thing about this piece of evidence is that Nietzsche refers to the "horrifying figure" as a frequent visitor. Here we can already see the specter of insanity looming over him, the materialization of the double of *Euphorion* with its commentary of satanic laughter, the terrible double of his bitter resentment that would help Nietzsche take revenge on the unattainable, absentee father, on Wagner, and on the God who had condemned him. Inspired by the author of *The Antichrist* and with a true novelist's intuition, Thomas Mann in *Doctor Faustus* made the career of his composer-hero depend on a pact with the devil, a pact concluded (or at least seriously attempted) not only by Nietzsche but by a vast section of European and Western culture.

Nietzsche, and much of the Western world with him, rebels against God because he hates and *envies* him.[21] Nietzsche's envy of God is not a simple psychological attitude on his part, it is, in biblical terms, the expression of mankind's constitutive wrong, the ancestral, ontological propensity to evil, no longer covered up in any way. Nietzsche's rebellion cannot be understood unless we understand the anthropologically objective, founding nature of Satan. *The Antichrist*, in its enormous pretensions (though not necessarily in its final significance), is a satanic work, it is a satanic interpretation of Christianity, with its history and message considered from Satan's viewpoint. Because Satan is the antichrist. The antichrist is Satan seeking to deceive and cover up his violence, duplicating himself in a false imitation of Christ once he realizes how Christ's revelation is spreading. Seeing that Christianity reveals and defends victims, the diabolical imitation of Christ transforms revelation of the victim into its violent mimicry, into the persecution of the persecutors.[22] All victims (and who cannot claim to be a victim in some respect?) cry out for revenge against their persecutors, real or alleged and mythically multiplied by category; and since the Christian message condemns all violence and all hypocritical concealment of violence, Christianity is fated to be, first and last, the sole target of this vindictive, hypocritical hatred. Nietzsche sensed the presence of this perverted imitation of Christ in his own times but mainly because, with the same demented logic as the will to power, he wanted to incarnate it at a higher level, at the very highest in fact, an endeavor that emerged later in the historically explosive form of Adolf Hitler, ex-social outcast, ex-scapegoat, who was determined to make scapegoats firstly of the Jews and then of Christianity. *The Antichrist* is the manifesto of the modern world's resentment of Christianity and the programmatic definition of the vaunted antichrist, the antichrist that was to be one and the same with Nietzsche himself.

All the essential points of the modern rejection of Christianity are to be found in *The Antichrist*: the Eucharist is assimilated to an archaic blood rite and denied any value as a matter evident in itself, the incarnation of the son of God is viewed as a shameful version of the Amphitryon story, the Church condemned as an institutionalized symbol of violence, Providence derided, the idea of immortality rejected, the Resurrection considered an invention of the early Christians, and a gross misunderstanding of the immaculate conception, mistaken for Christ's virginal birth and interpreted as sex-phobic sublimation. Many of these points had already appeared in a condensed form in *Human, All Too Human*,[23] but what is most interesting here is that Nietzsche now came to deny one of his greatest discoveries, contradicting himself as a consequence—the discovery of the difference between Dionysus and Christ, the same difference that Girard would later explore in a more proper way. In carrying out his rebellion against God, Nietzsche did not hesitate to destroy what would have assured his greatness and, above all, could have saved him. The philosopher-Ahab was now preparing to move in for the kill, to make his final assault on what he regarded as a hateful prey; and as he approached nearer, it showed itself to be strangely polymorphic and elusive, looking more and more like Dionysus, Proteus, the long-desired god of metamorphosis.

He Will Crawl to the Cross

The decisive moment when Nietzsche came to the point of denying himself in order to gain an advantage over his elusive opponent can be recognized in the central part of *The Antichrist*. In chapters 40–41, the philosopher-antichrist imagined the reactions of Christ's disciples, highly resentful at what he defines as the "most atrocious paradox" of the crucifixion, which makes it perfectly clear to us that the crucifixion lies at the very center of the crisis of the doubles in Nietzsche's mind. The "most atrocious" paradox is the one that redoubles and multiplies 'atrocities,' the paradox, that is, from which there is no escape:

> It was after this that an absurd problem emerged: "how could God permit it!" The troubled minds of the little community found an answer of truly frightful absurdity: God gave his son for the remission of sin, as a *victim*. All of a sudden it was the end of the Gospels! *Expiatory sacrifice*, and in its most repulsive, most barbaric form, the sacrifice of the *innocent* for the sins of the wicked! What horrifying paganism![24]

Nietzsche does not deny the uniqueness of the Gospel message but denies that it has anything to do with the death of Christ. Having performed this amputation, completely arbitrary but necessary for his purposes, the interpretation of the centrality of the death of Christ could be attributed to the disciples. And here Nietzsche started to discover for himself the significance of the "most atrocious paradox" of the crucifixion. The disciples solve their "absurd" problem with, in Nietzsche's words, "an answer of truly frightful absurdity," namely, the sacrifice of Jesus as an expiatory victim to satisfy his Father's idea of justice. Nietzsche was really referring to the theory of satisfaction or vicarious substitution, a theory evolved many centuries after the age of the apostles as an attempt to provide a logical and theological explanation for various aspects of Christ's death. It was a historical expression of Christian thinking made in ignorance of the anthropological dimension, from which it nevertheless derived, but Nietzsche, like many anti-Christians (and sacrificial Christians) of our own day, willfully misconstrued it literally, turning it on its head to attribute sacrificial violence to God the Father.[25]

But the most remarkable feature is his accusation that the apostles interpreted Christ's death in terms of sacrifice and violence, reflecting, as he says in chapter 40, "the least evangelical sentiment, *revenge*."[26] A sensational but inevitable admission, which enables us to see the reasons why the more prudent and elusive Heidegger stayed clear of the forbidden area into which the aspiring antichrist ventured. To be rid of the Christians Nietzsche needed to concentrate all the violence in them, all the will for vengeance, but in order to do it he was forced to admit that revenge is completely extraneous to the Gospels, forced to adopt the gospel viewpoint *without realizing the implications of his admission.* The contradiction is at once palpable if we remember that the type of sacrifice, attributed by him to the apostles' will for revenge and arousing his indignation here, is the same sacrifice that fired a bestial enthusiasm in him when done in the name of Dionysus: "*Expiatory sacrifice* [. . .] in its most repulsive, most barbaric form, the sacrifice of the *innocent* for the sins of the wicked! What horrifying paganism!" The philosopher or, if you prefer, his text has just an inkling that *all* the victims of Dionysus are innocent; at any rate, they are not guilty of the enormous wrongs for which they are blamed by the hate-filled mob. This had already been said by Nietzsche in more lucid moments of victimary insight but he had not drawn the conclusions that he should have done.

He recognized that the sacrifice of an innocent victim was something repulsive and barbaric, something horrifically pagan. The point is that sacrifice of the Dionysian type excluded the very awareness that, in spite of all his wriggling, he was unable to transfigure into the new form of a superhuman, divine state. His confusion of the Eucharist with the bloody rites of archaic and mystery cults, a mistake repeated by many in the modern world, could only backfire on himself because it is precisely the flesh and blood of the Eucharist that shows the stuff of all human rites, the stuff that man is made of. The Eucharist anticipates and performs in reality, in the form of a *rite*, what the Passion of Christ shows in history and in knowledge, causing them to emerge from *myth*.[27] The aspiring antichrist could only remain deaf and blind at the incandescent core of the difference that he had intuited and forced into the open, a sacrificial core that puts man in contact with God through the real repetition of his history, origin, and guilt. But to understand the sacrament at all would require virtues unknown to Nietzsche and to the typical modern intelligentsia: humility, obedience, acceptance, and

the ability to listen; in a word, the unconditional imitation of a good mediator, a mediator with no trace of hate or rivalry.[28] By refusing this imitation,
Nietzsche deprived himself of all defense against the satanic double that
from his earliest days he had felt to be behind him and within.

If Nietzsche came to touch on the pure and simple truth of the horror of Dionysus it was firstly because he wanted to fling it in the face of the
Christians to free himself not from sacrifice but from the moral awareness
of sacrifice, transforming this awareness into a mythological accusation
against the Christians to make them his scapegoat and divinize himself. But
once again, what was the sole source that enabled him to say what he did
say? Nietzsche's system of doubles always forces us back to the same basic
contradiction, because he himself constantly returned to it in his attempt to
escape from the trap of his own seeking, a trap that held him faster the more
he struggled. In the residual uniqueness that Nietzsche's divisive tactic con-
ceded to the Gospels, and no matter how well-hidden and compressed, the
difference remained; Nietzsche was unable to eliminate Christ's difference
in respect to Dionysus, and it reverberates in all his thinking and writing.
He refused to see that the minds of the Apostles reasoned as human minds
and, thanks to the experience of the Resurrection, were for the first time no
longer "troubled minds" since the apostles understood for the first time that
the point of view of the innocent victim was the opposite of the persecutors'
point of view.[29] What happened to the apostles after Christ's death, far from
being a moment of mental confusion, was the opposite of what was happening to Nietzsche; it was an authentic coming to their senses, that opened
their eyes to persecution and to their complicity in it; it was the event that
founded the Church and so clarified and strengthened a non-persecutory use
of human reason, which, like all man's cultural attributes, originated in the
violent reconciliation that the victim alone made possible.[30]

Nietzsche had understood the bloody origin of human reason quite
superbly when he intuited the presence, within the logical forms of knowledge, of a 'command,' an imperious, coercive act of the collective will, but he
excluded the existence of a command utilizing and overcoming man's violent
forms through forgiving them; he excluded a transcendent power that was
able to communicate and give orders to men because it revealed and sub-
verted their violent system. This use of human abilities in defense of the victims, of the defenseless, is the sacramental gift of the Holy Spirit, for which it

possesses the fundamental attribute of wisdom; and it is the only force that can give real, complete freedom from the doubles of violence. Nietzsche's attempt to trace it all back to a distortion of the early Christians backfired on him, because the facts spoke for themselves through his own words and intuitions. We can now understand the immediately following passage where he rejected the cognitive value and saving power of the Crucifixion, the real crux of the matter, for the struggle of the work as a whole, and for Nietzsche's mental stability.

St Paul was bound to be Nietzsche's chosen target; long an object of his hatred, he was now dubbed the "dysangelist." Envy, once again, offers a perfectly valid explanation for this: Nietzsche envied the personality of the mighty religious innovator that he had never succeeded in being, in spite of, or rather because of all his boastful bluster; but here, too, there is much more than a subjective grudge; there are objective causes that are most fully expressed in *The Antichrist*. They are the same causes that make St Paul an almost compulsory target for all anti-Christians who, in their attempt to nullify the Christian message, detach it from the figure of the founder and arbitrarily attribute the tradition stemming from Christ to the apostle. The anger felt by Nietzsche and his imitators is not unmotivated, since it was Paul who gave highly penetrating expression to the anthropological and historical significance of the Crucifixion, a formidable doctrine that Girard can help us to understand more fully.[31] The forces of Satan were hoping to silence forever the voice that had cried out against their power but, at the very moment of apparent triumph, Satan was defeated because the mechanism founding collective violence had been laid bare, that is, the secret mechanism of the devil, "murderer from the beginning." Satan, who finally comes to coincide with the Dionysus that Nietzsche glorified, had been literally fooled. This was the real reason for the genuine rage that seized Nietzsche whenever he mentioned St Paul, who predicted the "mystery of iniquity" of anyone who points to himself as God, which in the words of the apostle was equivalent to being the antichrist:[32]

> The "good news" is followed by the *worst of all*: Paul's. Paul incarnates the antithetical type to the "good news," the genius of hatred. *What* has he not sacrificed to hate, this dysangelist [*Dysangelist*]? First and foremost, the redeemer: he nailed him to *his* cross.[33]

To the eyes of the wrongdoer, the revelation of the wrong is the most serious wrong. For this reason, St Paul, who underlined the real meaning of Christ's crucifixion, was transformed and held responsible for it in Nietzsche's eyes. Execution by crucifixion, seen as just when carried out by the *imperium romanum*, became an unforgivable wrong now that St Paul was presumed responsible. Contradiction follows contradiction. The more Nietzsche tried to nail Christianity to the cross, the more he showed the reality, the *scandal of the cross*, as Paul puts it so admirably, taking a phrase straight from the Gospels that condenses the sense of the Christian message.[34]

It is no accident that Nietzsche omitted to quote this Pauline expression. In the face of the gospel doctrine of the *skandalon*, the stumbling block, he could do nothing but hold his tongue, and he was not alone in that, for, in Christ's teaching according to Girard's interpretation, the *skandalon* indicates the model that has become an obstacle in our path, the double bind of the rival who scandalizes us because we are secretly fascinated by him and since we are fascinated we are scandalized.[35] In fact, this was what Wagner had been for Nietzsche, what Christ was for him now and, together with Christ, every Christian. The final outcome of the *skandalon* is to kill the enemy who fascinates, to murder the victim on whom the scandal felt by everyone is concentrated. Thus scandal reveals its substantial identity with Satan. Satan is the *skandalon*, being the foundation of the system on which men's violent lives are based. The scandal of the cross, Nietzsche's scandal, is therefore Satan's reaction to the revelation of his hidden foundation. And in the last resort the scandal over the cross is the same as the scandal over the Church. To defend himself, Satan must break every visible link between the scandal of violent desire and the cross of Christ that is its result; he must shatter the revelation that sustains and guides the whole tradition, and disrupt its continuity to show that no tradition going back to Jesus Christ really exists.[36] But since this follows an identical logic to the insult of "idiot" directed at Christ *and* at all Christians, and originates in the same scandal that led to the crucifixion, it results in demonstrating the doctrine of the scandal. Whatever the scandalized person may do when faced with the revelation of his scandal, it can only confirm the existence of the scandal, it is inside him, it *is* him. Nietzsche is unable to cite or define the Pauline expression, because all he says and does is defined by it. And since the doctrine of the *skandalon*, in spite of two thousand years of incomprehension, can only derive from Christ and is no less a historical fact than the Crucifixion, it demonstrates the substantial continuity of what Paul says with the teachings of Christ.[37]

For this reason, falsifying theology and history so as to reduce Christianity to an invention of St Paul, rather than bringing relief to Nietzsche, poisoned him still further, causing him to exclaim in reference to the Gospels: "Fortunately those books are only literature for the most part . . ." (ch. 44).[38] The basic principle in biblical exegesis followed by most of the contemporary world could not be better expressed. Today's totally dismissive attitude, reducing the Bible to just another text and maybe considering it deplorably prolix, serious, and "politically incorrect," is so strong and influential that it has become law even for many biblical scholars.[39] Yet Nietzsche's relief when he remarked the prevalence of this tendency is somewhat suspect, and it should not make us overestimate the force of the 'literary' interpretation of the Bible that puts it on a par with any fable or myth (the same myths that are praised to the skies as long as they are not Christian myths). Why is it so 'fortunate' to consider the Gospels a literary epiphenomenon? Surely, their manifest falsehood had already been proclaimed? This good 'fortune' was to preserve the majority of people, for whom Nietzsche has suddenly become concerned, from some real danger. But from what? The nature of the danger that threatened Nietzsche himself is shown in ch. 53, after a mounting storm of anticlerical invective, accusing priests of what the writer feared and knew was in himself (memorable the "vampirism of wretched underground blood-suckers"[40]). Among so many insults, some criticism was bound to hit the mark for the simple reason that it repeated Christ's own strictures against the Pharisees in a subliminal, distorted way.

Nietzsche's intuition of the importance of the Crucifixion was so profound that, having reached this point of exasperation, he suggested quite clearly what Satan should have done, or rather should not have done, which was to crucify Christ! The fundamental passage is in the *First Epistle to the Corinthians* where Paul remarks that if the powers of this world had known what would happen, they would never have crucified Christ (2, 8). This passage was applied literally and most spectacularly in *The Antichrist*, but to understand it we must again penetrate the contradictions in the text, since Nietzsche had to be very careful to avoid direct, open denial. The contradiction that we saw before reappeared, but by fits and starts this time because the antichrist was now making his supreme effort at negation:

The conclusion of all idiots [*Der Schluss aller Idioten*], including women and ordinary folk, that a cause for which someone will face death (or, as with primitive Christianity, a cause that actually creates an epidemic of longing for death) has a certain value—this conclusion has proved a huge drawback to investigation, to the spirit of investigation and caution. Martyrs *harm* the truth . . . Even today, make persecution a little harsher and a sectarianism still insignificant in itself becomes *respectable.*—How? Perhaps the fact that someone sacrifices their life for a cause transforms its value? An error that has become respectable is an error with extra seductive charm: do you really believe, you theologians, that we would give you the chance to make martyrs with your lies? A cause is confuted by reverently placing it on ice—you also confute theologians in the same way . . . In the history of the world, the stupidity of all persecutors has been precisely that, namely, to make the cause of their adversaries appear honorable—presenting them with the appeal of martyrdom as a gift . . . A woman today will still go down on her knees before an error, because she has been told that someone was crucified for it. *Is crucifixion an argument then?*[41]

This text is a dramatic battlefield. Nietzsche tries to argue for rejecting the Crucifixion in general terms, referring to the stupidity of all persecutors "*in the history of the world*" (my italics). Obviously, since he was talking about Christians, he intended to refer to the persecutions of the early Christians but he would not and could not start with them since it would have meant underlining their uniqueness, which he had just denied. To demonstrate that the deaths of Christ and the martyrs were *just like all the others* he was obliged to talk about *all* the persecutors who had ever existed since mankind began, "from the foundation of the world" as the Gospel would say, but at this point the violence that he wanted to hide was revealed, in a truly genealogical way.

From his standpoint, there should be no reference to the persecutors of the victims *before* Christ, for the simple reason that they were not visible as human and historical persecutors, and he himself did not want them to be seen. They were the Thebans virtuously concerned to expel Oedipus and so get rid of the cause of the plague; they were the bacchantes possessed by Dionysus who tore their victim to pieces, murderers convinced that they killed in self-defense and because it was the will of the god. Their 'truth' is the subject matter of myth. Could Nietzsche have meant to say that no persecutor should have killed any victim? Certainly not, since Christianity says the same, while this philosopher-antichrist did his utmost to defend sacrifice, even human sacrifice. His problem was that, at that moment, the persecutors ought to have *returned* to invisibility as persecutors and, to this end, the Christian martyrs and, above all, their model, the crucified Christ, should not even have seen the light.[42]

What Nietzsche was speaking about, then, was the crucifixion, and what he wanted to incarnate, in accordance with previous promises and premonitions, was Satan's viewpoint as analyzed by St Paul. But, to alter the idiom slightly, this really amounted to letting the cross in through the door after he had secretly tried to throw it out of the window. Nietzsche was compelled to experience in his own person, at the expense of his already wavering mental stability, the triumph of the cross over Satan of which St Paul speaks. Once revealed for what he is, the victim can be denied no more: and there was nothing that the defender of Dionysus-Satan could do against this invincible truth. That was why D'Annunzio, though he remained fascinated by the dream of a pagan neo-foundation, recounted a story of failure in *The Flame of Life*, concluding the novel's alarming triangles with a reference to St Francis of Assisi; and the same failure occurs in *The Innocent* where Tullio Hermil does not manage to destroy the innocence of his intended victim. And it was also the reason why Thomas Mann, in spite of his high regard for Nietzsche, was almost compelled to describe without dissembling the stench and bloodiness of Dionysus and was unable to concur in Nietzsche's furious attack on Judeo-Christian morals and tradition.[43] In order to cancel out the event that revealed the victim, in all its uniqueness, the unsuccessful antichrist is forced to make visible all the other victims "in the history of the world." The sacrifice of the Christian martyrs demonstrates, *shows*, just that: it was murder and nothing else. Therefore Nietzsche sought to transform it into morbid self-sacrifice, into suicide substantially, without realizing the blatant contradiction with his criticism of the slaughterers for killing the martyrs. The morbid self-sacrifice that he attributed to the martyrs was really a projection of what he himself was about to do: to commit mental suicide, to do violence to himself as his last chance to fight the duel, to achieve the impossible sacrifice, a real, hysterical martyrdom of violence.

Martyr comes from the Greek meaning *witness*; with the example of Christ before them, martyrs bore witness to the truth of the victim; if necessary, they took the place of the victim, if, that is, it was the only way to ensure that the truth of the victim was not obliterated. Nothing could be further from the morbid desire for martyrdom, the "epidemic of longing for death," that Nietzsche attributed to the martyrs, obscuring the far more real imitative contagion of their killers or of those who stood by and cheered as the martyrs were killed. When the antichrist said that martyrs "*harm* the truth," he was referring to the damaged, substantially destroyed, 'truth' of myth (the new myth that Nietzsche had in mind), to the conviction of the persecutors, never again to recover its unanimity, and to the murderous, smiling mask of Dionysus, futilely substituted by an icy surface in Nietzsche's text. He would have liked to reduce the "honorable" aspect and "appeal of martyrdom" to just a matter of appearance when, to the contrary, it expresses the sole manifestation of good and of right knowledge, once things have been revealed for what they are. For years Nietzsche had directed more or less subtle criticisms against representations, while presenting himself as a champion of the *innocence* of appearances. His precise aim was to prevent our belief in representations that make us see the (guilty) desire and the (innocent) victim concealed by the mask; at the same time he extolled representations when they were presented as insuperable phenomena, that is to say, as masks taken for real while knowing that they are masks. From what real misdeed should this contradictory 'innocence of appearances' preserve us? Had not Nietzsche himself identified the violent origin of all our knowledge? Once again he had to forget, and make us forget, the value of his own discoveries. Instead, we must ask ourselves once more, and in a specifically epistemological sense this time, what was the secret knowledge, the hidden certainty, that made possible his penetrating diagnoses, whose consequences he would have been most reluctant to draw?

What enabled Nietzsche to grasp the violence underlying human representations, as we can understand perfectly well, was the fact that there exists only one absolutely true representation, one representation that coincides absolutely with the reality represented, a 'reality-representation' that is alone in totally rejecting all violence: the representation of the victim seen as completely innocent, of Christ dying on the cross and rising from the dead. This revelation confronts us with something beyond measure that no longer depends on us because we ourselves—with all that we are, all that we think and do—derive from it: whatever we may do can only confirm a revelation that appears not to come from ourselves. The simplicity of this observation is disarming, and yet invincible: the victim revealed in Christ is absolutely undeniable, because to deny him would be to kill another victim, to crucify Christ again.[44] Nothing human can touch the revealed truth: once enunciated, once given to men, it is irrevocable, eternal. The crucifixion *is* an argument, it is the source of every argument, the source of all knowledge, of all salvation. The woman who falls on her knees would have much to teach the wise philosopher who is about to be made mad by his distorted wisdom, human wisdom, the wisdom of persecutors conceived for other persecutors.

Erwin Rohde, in a letter to Overbeck in 1886, expressed his moral disgust for what Nietzsche maintained, and predicted: "He will crawl to the foot of the *cross*,"[45] but with his superior intelligence and humanistic conceit, he was far above imagining what a revealing, horrific crawling would result from the confrontation pursued by his erstwhile friend. Certainly, Nietzsche was to crawl to the cross, though he thought to do this in the manner of the serpent that tempted Eve: a repetition of original sin that started him off towards the final breakdown.

Immediately after the passage about the crucifixion in *The Antichrist*, the megalomania that should have shown Dionysus triumphant returned with the most disastrous consequences. In the face of the one real difference that dominated all the illusory differences concerning violence, the lover of Dionysus reaffirmed *his* difference, the raving difference of Zarathustra. This was the tragic signal of the approaching end. Like the trapped Ahab persistently lashing out at the monster dragging him down into the depths, or like the black flag of despair planted on Baudelaire's skull, the crisis of the doubles now reigned triumphant in Nietzsche's mind:

> But about all these things only one person spoke the word whose need had been felt for thousands of years—*Zarathustra*.[46]

At the beginning of *The Antichrist* Nietzsche had exclaimed, scandalized: "Almost two thousand years and not a single new God!"[47] That, then, was "the word whose need had been felt for thousands of years," the word of the myth, the *logos* of sacrificial neo-foundation, with the would-be biblical imitation of *Thus Spake Zarathustra* as its major classic, its oracular revelation. But the sheer physical presence of the martyrs, of the witnesses to violence, still stubbornly stood in the way of his proclaimed neo-foundation. Nietzsche could find nothing better with which to neutralize them than self-quotation, and clung to his illusory Bible, *Zarathustra*:

> Signs in blood they wrote as they travelled along, and their stupidity taught that the truth would be demonstrated with blood. But blood is the worst witness to truth; blood poisons even the purest doctrine and transforms it into delirium and heartfelt hatred.[48]

The blood of the martyrs persists in poisoning "even the purest doctrine," that is, the doctrine of Dionysus-Zarathustra with its dream of a new form of ancient ritual purity, since, in those far-off times, they certainly knew all about purifying, destroying blood. That blood was indelibly fixed in Nietzsche's mind, like poison. And the poison is blamed for the delirium and heartfelt hatred that convulses Zarathustra so tremendously, such as occurred during ancient crises if the violence remained visible and was not transfigured into the unanimous violence of sacrifice. A still more radical remedy had to be found, to beat the martyrs on their own ground, to fully achieve what they had undone. The supreme holocaust, so often evoked in the past, was about to be performed directly, revealing the real significance of the succeeding lines in the quotation from *Zarathustra*:

> And if you go through fire for the good of your doctrine—whatever does it prove! It means more if your doctrine comes from being burned at the stake.

With these words Dionysus-Zarathustra sealed his own fate. The only way to destroy the cross and its ineradicable, inescapable moral awareness was for Nietzsche to embody the sacrificial foundation, to realize in himself the 'death of God' that he had prophesied, to deliver himself up body and soul to the devil on his heels. A deliberate self-immolation will demonstrate the divine nature of the priest-king. And so all doubts will finally be removed and purity attained.[49]

This conclusion was already clearly contained in the inflationary strategy that leads to mass extermination: in the end, the greatly desired will to power had to lead to sacrifice, not so much the sacrifice of the detested 'weaklings' as of the aristocrats, potential rivals of the *one and only* superman but also best-suited, as victims, for the most serious crises calling for the most powerful and prestigious victims. And what crisis was more serious for Nietzsche than this? Only he could handle it, by his self-immolation: only "in sacrificing its finest specimens" could the Dionysian will "delight in its own inexhaustible nature."[50] The sacrifice would be perfect only when the last inhabitant of Olympus killed himself: and the Wagnerian-Nietzschean Walhalla went up in flames. Nietzsche could not forget that the mask is a mask, and decided to torch himself along with it.[51] Dionysus-Zarathustra, seeking to convince himself of his own divine nature, to show that he was the word awaited for two thousand years, decided to repeat the anthropological process leading to divinization.

The doctrine that comes "from being burned at the stake" may be seen as the exact opposite of the doctrine of the burning bush in which God appeared to Moses; it is the sacrificial pyre on which the victim was burnt and that then expressed his light, his divine nature, and taught how to kill other victims. This brings to mind Heidegger's glorification of fire in his political speeches during his rectorship at the beginning of the Nazi era, a fire which was more sinister than the disturbing, but after all still humanistic, flame that forms the title of D'Annunzio's novel.[52] Not yet fully satisfied by his 'millenary' affirmation of the Bible of *Zarathustra*, a few pages further on Nietzsche set the Indian codex of Manu in opposition to the Bible, with the words "over the whole book stands the *sun*,"[53] the same fiery sun that shone at the center of the labyrinth, the sacrificial star whose children are Thomas Mann's Hellenes, now shone over the "high noon" of Zarathustra and Dionysus. Having approached the sun of sacrifice too closely, Icarus-Nietzsche crashed into the sea of the doubles of insanity and drowned. The center had been reached, the sacrifice completed.

The book ends a few chapters later in a wild succession of exaggerated enthusiasm, accusation and cursing. In the *Law against Christianity*, intended to mark the start of the new era of salvation, and dated September 30, 1888 according to the "false chronology," the seventh and last proposition concludes: "The rest follows from that." A good deal of the history and culture of the twentieth century can be included in that "rest."

What None Have Perceived

Oh, lonely death on lonely life! Oh, now I feel my topmost greatness lies in my topmost grief.

—Ahab in *Moby Dick*[1]

What was there in the "rest" that followed from the *Law against Christianity*, regarding the fate of the unfortunate antichrist? There was madness, obviously, ". . . the vision of a feast [*Festes*] that I have yet to experience . . . ," as Nietzsche declared in *Ecce Homo*,[2] but not only that. By way of comment on concluding *The Antichrist* he wrote, again in *Ecce Homo*: "30 September great victory; seventh day; a god takes his ease beside the river Po."[3] Here, the seventh proposition of the *Law against Christianity* has become the seventh day, in an obvious allusion to the Bible: having created his "transvaluation of all values" the God-Nietzsche rested on the banks of the river. As he wrote to Carl Fuchs on December 11: "I cannot tell you *everything* that has been accomplished. In the next few years the world will be turned upside down: after the old God has been discharged, it'll be *me* who rules the world."[4] Now firmly in the grip of his deranged divinization transference, Zarathustra deluded himself in thinking he could enjoy his new status. But the eagerly awaited festivities were soon to reveal their most ancient nature, as a sacrificial feast.

And, in fact, it was on the banks of the Po that the drama took place, the final festivities. Some of the most important texts written by Nietzsche while insane, perhaps the most important, were rashly destroyed by his sister, Elisabeth. Luckily, however, among much sentimental invention intended to minimize her brother's madness, and long accepted as gospel truth by many people, she records what these pages contained:

> . . . he wrote some pages filled with strange imaginings, where the legend of Dionysus-Zagreus is mixed up with the Passion in the Gospels and with the contemporary personalities who were closest to him: the God, torn to pieces by his enemies and risen from the dead, walks along the banks of the Po and now sees below him everything he loved, his ideals, above all the ideals of the present period. His friends and fellow men have become his enemies and torn him to pieces. These pages are directed against Richard Wagner, Schopenhauer, Bismarck and his closest friends: Professor Overbeck, Peter Gast, Frau Cosima, my husband, my mother and myself.[5]

There can be no doubt about the substantial authenticity of this summary. We can reconstruct Nietzsche's conclusive thinking, in a similar way to the pre-Socratic fragments that he loved so much, as we shall see with two other important texts. Enveloped by madness, like Aschenbach by the cholera infecting Venice and his dreams, Nietzsche-Dionysus sees his destiny of dismemberment, his *sparagmós*, faithfully reproduced by the psychic dismembering of his mind. Zagreus is the ancient name for the Cretan Dionysus, from which in all probability the Greek Dionysus originated: Nietzsche's two-pronged probing, anthropological and personal, continues even now, reaching extreme clarity. Dionysus-Nietzsche's dismemberment takes place at the hands of all his friends, his relations, and the entire surrounding community. It is only now, when it is too late, that the collective aspect of sacrifice emerges fully, bringing to life the nightmares of Thomas Mann's characters.

It was not only a persecution delirium. Little by little, in the course of his painful existence, Nietzsche had been effectively abandoned by all his friends, even late in life when his letters clearly betray desperate loneliness.[6] Though he greatly admired pitilessness in his mythology, Nietzsche knew what it was to be shown no pity at his own expense and, on his best form, managed to show none himself. Examples are scattered throughout his writings, such as: ". . . indisputable lack of *suitable* company."[7] Other examples show us the recurrent images of the wayfarer and the dancer but the contexts take away all their transfiguring sparkle: "A weary wayfarer greeted by the harsh snarling of a dog"; "I'm looking for an animal that dances as my music wants and just a tiny bit—loves me. . . ."[8] This wayfarer was already exhausted in 1869, when Nietzsche wrote to Rohde:

> But friendship! There are people who doubt it exists. Certainly, it is a refined delicacy enjoyed by the few, by those exhausted wayfarers for whom life is just a journey across a desert . . .[9]

A kind of unreflecting, subliminal awareness runs throughout the life and works of this man, like those sick people who know the disease that is going to kill them and at the same time hide it from themselves. This circumstance makes Nietzsche's declarations about his good health and happiness excruciatingly painful, and their real diseased nature did not elude the infallible instinct of Mann and D'Annunzio. There is a precise sequence in the passage of the letter to Rohde about friendship: first the doubt surfaces, then comes the elitist "refined delicacy" illusory in nature, and finally the desert where all began and all will end. Nietzsche was unwilling to realize that men fear those who go into deserts. Speaking about his last encounter with his friend, Rohde said: ". . . he was surrounded by an indescribable atmosphere of *alienation from our world* [*Fremdheit*], something deeply *disquieting* [*Unheimliches*] for me. . . ."[10]

In order to be sincere about himself Nietzsche needed to momentarily relax his lethal self-control; for example, his distress over the failure of the triangle with Rée and Salomé led him to take a hefty sleeping draught and he managed to write to the other two:

> Bear in mind, both of you, that I am, after all, half-mad (*Halb-Irrenhäusler*) and suffer from migraine, my brain completely upset by loneliness. I come to that, and I consider it a reasonable assessment of the situation, after

taking an enormous dose of opium *in desperation*. But instead of losing my mind, it seems I am finally *regaining* it.[11]

Back to his senses once more, unfortunately, he wrote to Rée a few days later: "... don't confuse my rational mind [*Vernunft*] with the foolish things [*Unsinn*] I wrote in my last letter under the influence of opium. I am not at all mad, and do not even suffer from megalomania ... ,"[12] but he admits to Overbeck: "... I stretch every fiber of my being in the effort to control myself [*Selbst-Überwindung*]—but I have lived alone for too long, wearing myself out inside...."[13]

Further examples might be quoted. Otto Weininger provides what is perhaps the best commentary with the following observations, as long as we take "religion" to mean, not so much Christianity in general, as Christian consolation:

> Nietzsche's decline is explained by the absence of religion. [...] What he lacked was *grace*; and without grace, loneliness, even Zarathustra's loneliness, is intolerable.[14]

In 1883, in the enervating grip of mood swings, alternating between megalomania and an "implacable thirst for revenge" provoked by the humiliations received in his affective and social life, Zarathustra confessed, again to Overbeck: "*this* inner conflict [*dieser* Conflict in mir] is bringing me gradually closer to *madness*, I feel it most terribly...."[15] As he approached the end of his walk through the desert, the wayfarer came out with some desolate statements:

> I have never complained about my indescribable privations: never to hear a sound akin to me, never to sense suffering and desire like mine.[16]

Nietzsche's privations were "indescribable" above all else because he had deprived himself of the language of love and compassion capable of giving expression to them, but the fact remains undeniable that none of his friends or admirers understood, or wanted to understand, the desperate plea for love hidden behind Zarathustra's reckless skirmishes. Nobody had been the object of Ahab's love, consequently nobody loved Ahab. Evidently, this was

the bitter proof of the truth of Nietzsche's diagnosis of mankind as composed of cannibals. How can we gloss over the fact that, if he was abandoned,
it was also because nobody had the courage to recognize the enormous problems that he tackled alone? How can we silently pass over this concealment,
more hypocritical and cowardly than the reckless and, in its crazy way, honest
defiance thrown out by Nietzsche? For almost all of Nietzsche's admirers this
concealment took the form of blindness to the sense and significance of his
fate, depressingly confirming a prophecy about the lynching of great men
made by Nietzsche the 'psychologist.' The writings of Nietzsche are full of
premonitions that acquire the status of indictments when seen against the
background of this blindness, this collective insensibility:

> I really ought to have a circle of profound and sensitive people around me,
> to protect me, as it were, from myself, and who knew how to cheer me up
> as well: since someone who thinks the things that I have to, is always in
> imminent danger of self-destruction.[17]

As madness came closer, the signals of a Nietzsche who did not want
to die to himself continued to pass through the ever-thickening mask, or
rather through the funeral pile of masks, through the mask-tomb that was
suffocating him. Now and again in *Ecce Homo* there are terrible flashes of
human truths, shining through a thick veil of references and multiple levels
of interpretation: "All of my *Zarathustra* is a dithyramb to solitude or, if
anybody has understood it, to *purity* . . . And not to *pure madness*, fortunately."[18] The *pure madness* is obviously the madness of Parsifal, the "pure
madman," but this umpteenth attack on Wagner, at the same time an attack
on Christ, now becomes a description, vainly exorcized, of what was happening to the writer for these precise reasons. Another passage sums up a
recurrent series of reflections and prophecies: "You pay dearly for immortality. . . ."[19] One phrase is particularly striking: "I cannot do otherwise. So help
me God! Amen." The expression echoes Luther's celebrated words when
he refused to make his retraction at the Diet of Worms, and had already
been utilized in *Thus Spake Zarathustra*; it appears at the end of the poem
entitled *Unter Töchtern der Wüste* [*Among the Daughters of the Desert*], in
an apparently ironical and playful context, followed, however, by a close
that is also the start of the real poetic text: "The desert grows: beware all

those who conceal deserts within themselves!"[20] And in writing to Gast about *Ecce Homo*, he wrote: "I don't see, now, why I should bring on too fast the *tragic* catastrophe to my life, that begins with *Ecce*."[21] In vain he tried to delay "the *tragic* catastrophe" that had actually begun with *The Antichrist*. In a way not unlike Luther, Nietzsche the 'heretic,' the 'schismatic,' knew how to make a clean break, to take on himself an immense responsibility, and was secretly greatly afflicted by a growing sense of guilt, while he tried to shift the blame on to his hated adversaries (Christ, Luther himself, and the German nation as a whole). He was unwilling to see the wasteland being created around him, and was prepared to destroy himself rather than make the unprecedented admission. The growing desert was about to devour he who concealed deserts within himself.

All the motives for Nietzsche's prescience and self-destructive urge are found condensed in one of his last poems, *Zwischen Raubvögeln* [*Among Birds of Prey*]. Here we are shown the desired and dreaded face hiding behind the desperate erotic metaphors of *Among the Daughters of the Desert*, who are correctly recognized by Thomas Mann as the "figures covered by veils and frills" of the Cologne brothel, ghosts of a manliness never attained. In the light of what has been said, the text could almost speak for itself as proof of the fundamental importance, which is to say the real greatness of this failed prophet, of his poetry, and of the truth that he tried to suppress, a truth liberated more easily in song, as another poet, D'Annunzio, understood in his ode *Per la morte di un distruttore* [*For the Death of a Destroyer*]. Here is the central part and the conclusion of *Among Birds of Prey*, that can be considered as Nietzsche's testament-poem:

> Now—alone with yourself,
> a pair with your knowledge,
> among a hundred mirrors
> false before yourself,
> among a hundred memories,
> uncertain, tired with every injury,
> cold with every frost,
> strangled with your own cord,

self-knower,
self-slaughterer!—

Why did you draw tight
the cord of your wisdom about you?
tempt yourself
into the paradise of the old serpent?
slither stealthily
into *yourself*—into *yourself*? . . .—A sick man now,
made ill by the poison of the serpent;
a prisoner now, you drew the toughest lot,
working your own pit
crouching,
opening a cave in yourself,
digging into yourself,
clumsy,
stiff,
a corpse—weighed down by a hundred burdens
overloaded with yourself,
someone *who knows!*
someone *who knows himself!*
the *wise* Zarathustra! . . .

You looked for the heaviest load
and found *yourself*—you cannot get rid of yourself . . .

Lying in wait,
huddled up,
someone who can no longer stand up!
Already you tangle with your tomb,
benumbed spirit . . . !
And but a moment ago so proud,
on all the crutches of your pride!
But a moment ago the man who lives alone without God,
who lives as a pair with the devil,
the scarlet prince of all arrogance! . . .

Now—between two nothings
bent,
a question mark,
a tired enigma—an enigma for *birds of prey* . . .

they will "undo" you, for sure,
they are already hungry for your "undoing,"
they already flap around you, their enigma,
around you, hanged man! . . .
O Zarathustra!
self-knower! . . .
self-slaughterer! . . .[22]

The Promethean vulture evoked by Nietzsche as a young man returns
here *en masse*.[23] These "birds of prey" are the feared "cannibals" of *Human,
All too Human*, the vultures all set to 'undo,' in the dual sense of the original
Greek verb *luein*, i.e. both to resolve and destroy, the enigma-Nietzsche; they
are the gravediggers of his posthumous glory all set to feed on his death, on
his flesh. The first verse of the quotation contains the generative image of
the doubles, that are created by the false consciousness of the imitator of an
actor, the clown-God ("the two of us with your knowledge [. . .] false before
you"), and then multiply to become the "hundred mirrors" and "hundred
memories" that now beset him and lead him to the end invoked in the poem.
Zarathustra crouching down, sick, in the pit, in the cave; Zarathustra hanged,
torn to pieces; Zarathustra buried. The most fitting comment would appear
to come from the hated Gospels: "Wheresoever the body is, thither will the
eagles be gathered together" (*Luke* 17, 37).[24]

For fear of falling into the grave that he had been the most eager to dig,
Nietzsche, like a trapped animal, grabs at whatever he can to save himself.
The italics in the text are like desperate props trying to shore up differences
in the doubles crisis of the madness destroying him. The same desperate
props are to be found in his posthumous writings in the form of obsessively
repeated daily prohibitions and prescriptions made at the time as he was
completing *The Antichrist*. In the following short sequence there can be no
doubt about Nietzsche's intention to throw back at Christianity the doubles
overwhelming his mind:

Don't wear glasses when you go out!
don't buy books!
don't go among crowds!
   [. . .]
Ch. on faith
Ch. on Paul
   ways to make people ill
   ways to make people *mad*[25]

"I cannot do otherwise. So help me God! Amen": the phrase from *Thus Spake Zarathustra*, repeated in *Ecce Homo*, should not appear out of context because Nietzsche in his madness was by now a whirling mass of words and symbols, where anything could indicate anything else but more revealingly than in lucid states of mind. We are bound, surely, to recognize a desperate prayer in this phrase? Men's relationship to God is not decided on the basis of simple words or simple external facts. That type of view is purely judgmental or sacrificial and has nothing to do with the Gospels; indeed, it would justify attacks of the sort made in *The Antichrist*. But, to be exact, such attacks would never have been necessary, since Christianity would never have survived beyond its infancy if there were no more to it than that. The real Christian attitude is shown by De Lubac when, in true Christian fashion, he recognizes the infinite causes for scandal that helped turn Nietzsche away from the Word, from the Bread of Life, and have also dissuaded many others with a similar outlook.[26]

What counts in relation to God is the individual's experience of reality that shapes his destiny, and sorrow and suffering are an important part. By bearing his suffering, Dionysus-Zagreus relives once again, after thousands of years, the real nature of his destiny. The revelation, denied in the manner of Lucifer, occurs: the scandalized becomes the scandal and the philosopher-king becomes the victim that he has always known himself to be. The story of the god who is torn to pieces is compounded "with the Passion in the Gospels," that is, with the Crucifixion and Resurrection of Christ. The difference between Dionysus and Christ returns but this time it comes to testify to the silent victory of the cross of Christ.[27] Nietzsche is the *Ecce Homo*, as Pilate designated Christ, the victim handed over to the mob that is going to crucify him, to tear him to pieces. Significantly, *Ecce Homo* was also the provisional title for *Parsifal*, Wagner's most Christian opera.[28] The union between the old rival and the new is now complete.

The quartering of Dionysus is revealed as equivalent to the crucifixion of Christ; the denier and envier of Christ is compelled to take Christ's place, to go along with the revelatory power of Christ's shameful death. Thomas Mann writes of the "agonizing spectacle of self-crucifixion"[29] but fails to understand its anthropological and spiritual significance, to grasp the truth that asserts itself despite and through the reckless strivings of Dionysus's champion. That truth is the truth of human origin. The simple form of the cross, which is central to Nietzsche's mental collapse, reproduces the four directions of *quartering* a human body, as effectively performed by the Dionysian mobs and again on so many other occasions in ancient and modern times.[30] This quartering is recorded in myths throughout the world wherever a divine being is torn to pieces and so gives origin to the four parts of the world or to the four cardinal points.[31] The form of the swastika offers some striking points of comparison: a solar and hierogamic symbol, it shows us the matrix of the labyrinth, the circular movement of the group as it closed round the victim to tear him to pieces; with Nazism, this archaic symbol became the modern symbol of the hell that only men know how to create for their fellows.[32] Mann separated what he defines as the philosopher's "infantile sadism"[33] from the large-scale organized sadism of the Nazi regime, and his distinction is no doubt right. But this must not become, as it became for most of Nietzsche's admirers, a form of denial of the glorification of violence shared by Nietzsche and a significant part of European culture. In the same way our refusal of that attitude must not become a denial of the problems that many intellectuals and politicians of that period deluded themselves in thinking that they could solve through such a glorification of violence.[34] Nazism was the continuation of the disease of the spirit present in Nietzsche, though the Nazis certainly went beyond anything imagined by Nietzsche in the vulgarity and brutal literalness with which they carried it out, sadly, far clearer than so many disquisitions. The Nazis transformed Nietzsche's opposition of Dionysus to Christ in their attempt to substitute the cross with the swastika, to bury the cross under the weight of their violence, under the awesome neo-foundation achieved through massive slaughter that Nietzsche had predicted. But the cross demystifies the swastika precisely because it represents what happens from an opposite point of view: every reassertion of the swastika can only reveal the truth of the cross, which is concealed in vain. The cross is the revealed center of the labyrinth-swastika evoked by Nietzsche, the labyrinth cave where he went to bury himself; the labyrinth, a symbol of the afterlife of great antiquity. And it is by bringing to light once more the death of the vanquished, the forgotten ones, of us all in the end, that the cross of Christ proclaims and re-establishes life itself, and points towards the empty tomb of the Resurrection.

By throwing himself into the tomb to bury himself, and into the fire to sacrifice himself, Nietzsche repeated as actions the fate of the now revealed victim whom he had tried to deny in words. The unsuccessful attempt to oppose Dionysus to Christ at the close of *Ecce Homo* ("–Have I been understood?—*Dionysus against the crucified Christ*"[35]) became a form of identity in the notes written in his madness, his final, definitive identity: he not only signed himself "The Crucified" but wrote to Cosima: "I too have been hanged on the cross. . . ."[36] This is not a questionable desire on my part to annex a feature of Christianity but the final emergence of a truth that was independent of the breakdown of a great mind and independent of subjective interpretations. Dionysus *is* Christ crucified because Christ crucified is the revelation, that wants to become salvation, of all victims killed in the name of Dionysus. There is a striking confirmation of this objective movement, already clearly recognizable in the extant notes and letters of madness.

Nietzsche's patent identification with Christ is expressed in a note written in Italian and sent to Jean Bourdeau in January 1889, now lost, that remains almost unknown in spite (or because?) of its obvious importance: "I am the Christ, Christ in person, Christ crucified."[37] This impressive crescendo, almost Trinitarian in its final utterance of a truth that he had always denied, clarifies and unifies, in a sense that I would define 'supererogatory,' all the references to being crucified or hanged on a cross scattered throughout the notes and letters of madness. Even the choice of Italian seems to convey this sudden coincidence with the principle itself of what Nietzsche previously hated, the Church, symbolically represented—as for other German intellectuals—by the southern country historically at the center of Catholicism; at the same time, he did not choose Latin, the official ecclesiastical language, probably because he wants to use the living liturgical language of his novel identity and glory.[38] A new era was beginning, the era of Dionysus become Antichrist and then, being crucified, simply and 'supererogatorily' *the* Christ, a Christological title that does not coincide with an inverted and Dionysiac Christ as suggested by some interpreters such as Janz.[39] Nietzsche, the madman announcing the death of God and finally expelled from the churches, has become this God and his living, collapsing Church, now one and the same with his mad prophet. If this is madness, as it is, there is in it the method of a real crucifixion.

In another extraordinary testimony, no less underrated and revelatory than the note to Bourdeau, Overbeck records that in Turin Nietzsche,

> pronouncing short phrases in an indescribable, subdued tone, was able to communicate things sublime, admirably prophetic and unspeakably horrific, about himself as the successor of the dead god [*über sich als den Nachfolger des toten Gottes*], accompanying his words with a kind of punctuation at the piano, and followed again by convulsions and attacks of unutterable pain. . . .[40]

This scene completes the destroyed fragment of Dionysus-Zagreus walking along the banks of the Po, and provides another essential nuance about Nietzsche as "successor of the dead god." It is an enigma to be solved, not unlike those of the god Apollo and Heraclitus, but with the additional drama of modern awareness. "Successor" means that we are now in the situation prophesized in the saying on the death of God by the phrase "Mustn't we become gods?" only applied here to the single person of the prophet. The "things sublime, admirably prophetic and unspeakably horrific" would refer to the definitive advent of the law of death and transfiguration of the eternal recurrence, but the already accomplished 'succession,' that Nietzsche tries to underline by his punctuation at the piano, breaks down and collapses into renewed "convulsions and attacks of unutterable pain," confirming the final identity of the 'successor-god' with the crucified God. No eternal recurrence will be able to cancel this irreversible condition. The unprecedented novelty of Dionysus's neo-foundation eventually becomes compatible with the infinite repetition of the pagan cycles in the person of its herald, nailed down to the truth he had never wanted to recognize. This contradiction, a true realization and refutation of the doctrine of eternal recurrence, emerges in the following words of Overbeck's testimony, where he explains that those were "rare and short moments," and that "what prevailed were declarations about the mission he attributed to himself, that of being the clown of the new eternities [*der Possenreißer der neunen Ewigkeiten*]."[41] The "new eternities" correspond to the spirals of the eternal recurrence, now irreversibly embodied in the crucified "clown" who had proclaimed them.

A famous incident occurred during Nietzsche's madness that may really make an emblematic conclusion for this examination of his life and ideas: Nietzsche saw (or he thought he saw[42]) a horse being beaten in the street and made an attempt to embrace it defensively.[43] The scene is made more vivid still by a literary parallel in *Crime and Punishment* (the nightmare of the pre-Nietzschean character of Raskolnikov[44]), which is, perhaps, alluded to in a letter and in one of the fragments.[45] Nietzsche must have sensed the truth of suffering in the beaten horse, such as he had long suffered himself and exorcized in the worst way: in the suffering of the substitute victim that he had long sought to have die in place of himself. Now that all is lost, he can recognize such suffering. It seems reasonable to conclude that this was the only way for him to have access to a feeling of compassion, so long denied. This compassion is not generically Schopenhauerian, as Verrecchia would seem to suggest.[46] Schopenhauer's compassion also draws more of its truth and *pathos* from Christianity than from Buddhism, even if the scandal of human violence led him to seek the truth in the remote and misty regions of the Orient and metaphysics rather than in his own violence. In its crazy paradoxical way, the compassion of Dionysus the Crucified can only be Christ's compassion. And this compassion goes well with some thoughts on the fate of a man who always refused Christ but remained on Calvary all his life, unconscious and unheeding, at the end proclaiming himself to be Christ crucified.

Was the philosopher-antichrist forgiven by Christ? Nobody can tell, of course. To be effective, forgiveness must be accepted. Jesus said that the sin against the Holy Ghost would not be forgiven,[47] not because it merited divine vengeance but because the sin consists precisely in refusing forgiveness. "It is a fearful thing to fall into the hands of the living God" because it is terrible to fall into the hands of this forgiving God and reject him.[48] And if Life, Love, and Forgiveness are denied, what possibilities for salvation remain? Wasn't it against the real possibility of being forgiven that Nietzsche struggled so strenuously? In that sense, his madness has none of

the madness of the Crucifixion.⁴⁹ But if the antichrist as *figura*, as the diabolical personification of anti-forgiveness, cannot by definition be forgiven, the
person who desperately, theatrically, incarnated the role could be, if there
remained in him something not reducible to sheer negation, to sheer death.

Finally, we will look at the last verses of *Glory and Eternity*, the Dionysian Dithyramb intended by Nietzsche to conclude *Ecce Homo*, and defined
by him in a letter to Gast "my supreme achievement [...], composed beyond
the seventh heaven [...]. One could die if read unprepared...."⁵⁰ Here, his
mysticism attains its finest expression, as D'Annunzio clearly recognized
when he quoted them in his ode on the death of Nietzsche. Certainly, this
is the mysticism of Dionysus and the eternal recurrence, since, just as there
exists a mysticism in union with the God of infinite love, so there exists a
mysticism of violence, sublimated or expressed. A sacrificial theory of the
origin of culture enables us to identify this mysticism as the primitive mysticism of the victim who was worshipped because he was divine. But is this
kind of demystification sufficient? I do not think so.

The systematic ambiguity of Nietzsche's doubles justifies us in thinking
that there could be something more here. Let us take the last three stanzas:

Supreme star of Being!
Table of eternal figures!
You come to me?—What none have perceived,
Your mute beauty—Why don't you flee from my sight?

Necessity's insignia!
Table of eternal figures!
—but you know already:
what everyone hates,
what *I* alone love,
that you are *eternal*!
That you are necessary!
My love is kindled eternally
only by necessity.

Necessity's insignia!
Supreme star of Being!

—never reached by desire,
never stained by no,
eternal yes of Being,
I am your yes eternally:
because I love you, o Eternity!—[51]

We need to ask ourselves two things: who comes so surprisingly to Nietzsche (*You* come to me?), and what is it that "none have perceived"? The demonstrative pronoun "what" recalls the demonstratives used by the mystical literature of all religions to indicate an absolute and eternal reality, that is to say, in the sacrificial terms that must be familiar to the reader by now, the victim expelled into the separate sphere of the sacred and therefore divinized. "Necessity's insignia" is in itself the insignia of sacrifice, the "supreme star of Being" is the victim-sun that shines only when transfigured by the ritual "insignia" of necessity, only when inserted in the "table of eternal figures." It would be a mistake to underestimate the religious force in these symbols of the divinizating transference but we are still within the sphere of the violent transfiguration up to this point, of unreflecting violence blindly believed to be divine. However, *something* remains in the text that cannot be entirely reduced to the anthropological scheme of man's origin.

The eternity and necessity that ought to guarantee the eternal recurrence are revealed as "*what everyone hates / what I alone love.*" He alone loves eternity, *all* the others hate it. The victimary scheme of all against one reappears, invincible. And since he identifies with eternity, it is the victimary scheme, yet again, that closes in on him to make him the ultimate, supreme victim.

This irrepressible victim who, after divinization, always returns immutably to visibility as victim, is the Christian God. Love is the only intermediary that can establish a relationship between Nietzsche and this unknown God, this strangely eternal and incarnate God, never reached by violent desire, "never stained by no." This stranger God, already invoked by Nietzsche in a poem written as a boy and dedicated to the unknown God,[52] reappears in *Zarathustra* through the projected *alter ego* of a sorcerer, who starts off the poem by saying: "Who will warm me, who loves me still?" Here again are the hunting images found at the beginning of this study, images that show us one last aspect, more profoundly sincere and painfully real:

... Do you want to come *within,*
Within my heart,
To reach inside, reach my most secret
Thoughts?
Impudent! Unknown—thief!
What do you want to steal?
What do you want to overhear?
What do you want to extort,
Torturer!
You—persecutor God!
Or must I, like a dog,
Roll over and over before you?
Devoted, beside myself with joy,
Wagging my tail for you—love?
In vain! You pierce me again,
Most cruel sting! No,
Not a dog—only your prey am I,
Most cruel hunter!
The proudest of your prisoners,
You, robber behind the clouds!
Speak, finally,
What do you want from *me*, bandit?
You, veiled by lightning! Stranger! Speak,
What do you *want*, stranger—God?—[...]
Ah! Ah!
And you torture me, madman that you are,
Annihilate my pride?
Give me love—who warms me still?
Who loves me still?—give warm hands,
Give heart-warming braziers,
Give to me, the loneliest of all,
Whom ice, ah! seven-fold ice
Teaches to crave for enemies,
Even enemies,
Give, or rather give in,

Most cruel enemy,
To me—*yourself!*—

Away!
And see, he too has fled,
My last and only companion,
My great enemy,
My stranger,
My persecutor God!—

Oh no! Come back,
With all your tortures!
To the last of all the lonely ones
Oh come back!
All my torrents of tears
Stream towards you!
And the last flame of my heart—Flares up for you!
Oh come back,
My stranger God! My sorrow! My ultimate—bliss![53]

Zarathustra failed to exorcize these tormented, splendid verses with his clumsy cave, nor with the forced idea of the last pope who roams the woods in search of the last-remaining devout Christian and mourns the loss of his God, suffocated "by his excessive compassion"; in the *Dionysian Dithyrambs* Nietzsche tried once more to neutralize the text with a coda in which Dionysus addresses Arianna with the words: "*I am your labyrinth.*"[54] Nietzsche's persistence in these efforts only shows their futility. The sorcerer's stranger God, this "most cruel" hunter, is the defenseless prey who reveals all the cruelty of the hunters, the ever-living God into whose hands it is terrible to fall, the lamb slaughtered by mankind who silently comes to judge in *Revelation*.[55]

"What none have perceived," the "mute beauty" that, unthinkably, does not flee from the sight of its worshipper because it is finally absolved from the transference of the violent divinizers, is the God of the victims, whose face is invisible to human beings because they are blinded by the mask of their violence and so unable to see it. In order to see it, they must bend their knee before the one who was humiliated and trampled on by all; they must recognize that there alone lies the blame, and there alone redemption.

But there are those who refuse to do this, who refuse to believe that they, too, have been forgiven; and so, in order to see, to embrace, this inaccessible God, they are reduced to madness.

Notes

Introduction. A Strange Debt to Europe

1. F. NIETZSCHE, *Sämtliche Briefe. Kritische Studienausgabe*, ed. G. Colli and M. Montinari, De Gruyter, Berlin-New York 1975–1984 (hereafter NSB), vol. 8, 573.

2. Translation by Charles Eliot Norton.

3. R. GIRARD, G. FORNARI, *Il caso Nietzsche. La ribellione fallita dell'Anticristo* [*The Nietzsche Case. The Failed Rebellion of the Antichrist*], Marietti: Genova-Milano 2002.

4. I remember well the manager of a university press exclaiming, after my explanation of the content of the book: "I don't believe *one* word of what you say!" It was September 2, 2001, at a political science convention in San Francisco, a few days before 9/11. I could not avoid a symbolic association afterward.

5. This anthology rightly includes the most important essay by Girard on Nietzsche: "Dionysus versus the Crucified," published in *Modern Language Notes* 99 (1984), 816–835, and re-published with the modified title "Nietzsche versus the Crucified" in *The Girard Reader*, ed. J. G. Williams, Crossroad, New York 1996, 243–261.

6. On this see chapter 2, note 14.

7. M. SILVESTRI, *La decadenza dell'Europa occidentale*, vol. 1, *Anni di trionfo 1890–1914*, Einaudi, Torino 1977, V.

8. *Acéphale* was a magazine founded by Bataille in the late '30s as a manifesto for *La conjuration sacrée* [*The Sacred Conspiracy*], a secret society inspired by Nietzsche and the idea of human sacrifice (this finally became, for Bataille, the idea of sacrificing himself, fortunately avoided at the last moment).

9. See R. GIRARD, *Achever Clausewitz. Entretiens avec Benoît Chantre*, Carnets Nord, Paris 2007,

particularly 308–327; R.GIRARD, *Battling to the End: Conversations with Benoît Chantre*, transl. by Mary Baker, Michigan State University Press: East Lansing 2010, 181–193.

10. On *Kultur* (*Cultur*) and *Zivilisation* (*Civilisation*) in Nietzsche see, e.g., F. NIETZSCHE, *Kritische Studienausgabe. Herausgegeben von Giorgio Colli und Mazzino Montinari*, De Gruyter, Berlin-New York 1999 (hereafter NKS, with the title of the quoted text); vol. 12, *Nachlaß 1885–1887*, 9[142], 416; and vol. 13, *Nachlaß 1887–1889*, 15[67], 451, and 16[10], 485–486.

11. See chapter 4, note 2, and chapter 5, note 35.

12. See chapter 5.

13. I began stressing this point in my subsequent interpretations of Nietzsche contained in G. FORNARI, *Da Dioniso a Cristo. Conoscenza e sacrificio nel mondo greco e nella civiltà occidentale* [*From Dionysus to Christ: Knowledge and Sacrifice in the Greek World and the Western Civilization*], Marietti, Genova-Milano 2006 (shortly to be published in English by Michigan State University Press) and *Filosofia di passione. Vittima e storicità radicale* [*Philosophy of Passion: Victim and Radical Historicity*], Transeuropa, Ancona-Massa 2006.

14. She excluded any "scapegoat theory" to explain the totalitarian persecution of the Jews, refusing to give them *a priori* a collective label of completely innocent victims, which would have precluded an objective analysis of the phenomenon (H. ARENDT, *The Origins of Totalitarianism*, Harvest Books, San Diego-New York-London 1976, 5–7); paradoxically, Arendt's inquiry proves to be useful precisely because it rejects an abstract, ideological scapegoat theory.

15. See G. FORNARI, "Figures of the Antichrist: The Apocalypse and Its Restraints in Contemporary Political Thought," in *Contagion: Journal of Violence, Mimesis, and Culture,* 2010 (17), 66–83.

16. It is interesting that the dilemma between *Kultur* and *Zivilisation* can be recognized today, at the level of international politics, in the contradiction between the traditional sovereignty of the nation State and the new idea of a global 'regime' based on the affirmation of human rights: both the alternatives have proved disastrous if we consider the old nationalism and the recent 'humanitarian' wars exploiting human rights as a moral pretext for the particular interests of single great powers.

17. F. NIETZSCHE, *Werke. Kritische Gesamtausgabe begründet von Giorgio Colli und Mazzino Montinari, weitergeführt von Volker Gerhardt, Norbert Miller, Wolfgang Müller-Lauter und Karl Pestalozzi*, De Gruyter, Berlin-New York 1999 (hereafter NW), I, 1, 1[71Z], 95.

Chapter 1. The Hunt for the Whale

1. H. MELVILLE, *The Works. Standard Edition*, vol. 7, *Moby Dick or, The Whale*, Russell & Russell, New York 1963, 2, 368.

2. ["Uniqueness" is not to be intended in rivalrous opposition to the other religions, beginning with Judaism from which Christianity arose.]

3. [See G. VATTIMO, *Le avventure della differenza. Che cosa significa pensare dopo Nietzsche e Heidegger*, Garzanti, Milano 1980, 71 ff.]

4. M. HEIDEGGER, *Holzwege*, Klostermann, Frankfurt am Main 2003, 249.

5. [More recently Vattimo, in the wake of Girard, with admirable honesty has changed his attitude towards Christianity, but without giving up his 'postmodern' view of Nietzsche, that in my opinion misses the tragical core of his thought.]

6. NKS, vol. 6, *Götzen-Dämmerung*, 65.

7. NKS, vol. 6, *Ecce homo*, 365.

8. NKS, vol. 13, *Nachlaß 1887–1889*, 25[6], 639–640.

9. R. CALASSO, "*Monologo fatale*," in F. NIETZSCHE, *Ecce homo*, ed. R. Calasso, Adelphi, Milan 1970, 162.

10. Nietzsche's opposition of paganism to Christianity inspired me to write *Fra Dioniso e Cristo. La sapienza sacrificale greca e la civiltà occidentale* [*Between Dionysus and Christ: The Greek Sacrificial Knowledge and the Western Civilization*], Pitagora, Bologna 2001. The present study is the continuation and provisional conclusion to that work. [My interpretative work was continued in the second edition of my book, soon to be published in English: *Da Dioniso a Cristo. Conoscenza e sacrificio nel mondo greco e nella civiltà occidentale*, Marietti, Genova-Milano 2006. The new title, modified from a dilemma to a transformation, intends to stress both the discontinuity and the continuity between Christianity and sacrificial religion.]

11. [I wrote the first version of these lines under the influence of Girard's evaluations, but we should not forget that the Latin motto *Bene navigavi, cum naufragium feci* (I made a good voyage, as I was shipwrecked), used by Nietzsche in *The Case of Wagner* to describe Wagner's fatal failure due to adopting Schopenhauer's pessimism (NKS, vol. 6, *Der Fall Wagner*, 20; from a Latin translation of Diogenes Laertius quoted by Schopenhauer: NKS, vol. 14, *Kommentar*, 404), must be applied to his own fatal voyage, as he himself indirectly did in a fragment describing the 'eternal present' in which he thought he lived (NKS, vol. 13, *Nachlaß 1887–1889*, 16[44], 501; cf. letter to Georg Brandes of May 23, 1888; NSB, vol. 8, 317–319). The final reference is to the truth made visible by this wreck, and inaccessible to whoever remains in a safer harbor.]

Chapter 2. The Eternal Recurrence of Madness

1. A. VERRECCHIA, *La catastrofe di Nietzsche a Torino*, Einaudi, Turin 1978, 261–270 [the wrong data on syphilitic infection recorded in the clinical journals of Basel and Jena are due either to a groundless rumor or to declarations of Nietzsche himself, who perhaps wanted to boast about his sexual activism]. The syphilis theory is confuted in detail in a more recent Italian biography of Nietzsche, M. FINI, *Nietzsche. L'apolide dell'esistenza*, Marsilio, Venice 2002 (365–371), a lively, richly informative work which has the merit of going against the idealized, hypocritical image of Nietzsche the man, even if it repeats some typical clichés about his ideas.

2. The moralistic, managerial Elisabeth would not accept syphilis as an explanation: her theory was that her brother's madness was due to abuse of sleeping draughts, though he had in fact given them up years before (M. FINI, *Nietzsche*, cit., 371–372).

3. T. MANN, "Nietzsche's Philosophie im Lichte unserer Erfahrung," in *Schriften und Reden zur Literatur, Kunst und Philosophie*, vol. 3, Fischer Bücherei, Frankfurt am Main-Hamburg 1968, 23–24.

4. Supporters of the idea of syphilitic insanity are forced to extend the period of latency of the disease beyond all medical probability, *vacatio imperii* that has become the *raison d'être* of the idea as it is used pro-Nietzsche.

5. On this denomination see C.P. JANZ, *Friedrich Nietzsche. Biographie*, vol. 3, Carl Hansen Verlag, München-Wien 1979, 35–36.

6. [An exception was a recent acquaintance of Nietzsche, August Strindberg, a literary genius, who wrote to him in Latin on December 31, 1888: "Litteras tuas non sine perturbatione accepi …"

("I received your letters not without some perturbation . . .") ; F. NIETZSCHE, Briefwechsel. Kritische Gesamtausgabe, ed. G. Colli and M. Montinari, De Gruyter, Berlin–New York 1975–2004 (hardcover edition, from now on NB), III, 6, 414. After answering Nietzsche Strindberg wrote to the Danish critic Georg Brandes, a new admirer of the philosopher, enclosing three letters just received from Nietzsche: "Jetzt glaube ich, daß unser Freund Nietzsche verrückt ist . . ." ("Now I believe that our friend Nietzsche is mad . . .") and concluding with an eloquent: "Was thun [= tun]?" ("What has to be done?"); NB , III, 7/3, 2, 1102.]

7. Letter of January 4, 1889 (NSB, vol. 8, 575).

8. Letter of January 9, 1889 (NB, III, 6, 419–421). Cf. A. VERRECCHIA, *La catastrofe*, cit., 180.

9. Gast, who even owes the name by which he is best known to Nietzsche (his real name was Johann Heinrich Köselitz), was only the first of many to fall knowingly under the influence of Nietzsche. Even when he visited Nietzsche in the mental asylum he still refused for some time to admit the evidence of his own eyes (M. FINI, *Nietzsche*, cit., 356). To tell the truth, among all the fanatics, misfits, and opportunists who came Nietzsche's way, Gast remains the most attractive and the one who paid most dearly in personal terms. In the end, poor Gast had to revise his opinion about his master when he found out that Nietzsche held him in contempt.

10. Cf. F. OVERBECK, *Erinnerungen an Friedrich Nietzsche, mit Briefen an Heinrich Köselitz (Peter Gast) und einem Essay von Heinrich Detering*, Berenberg, Berlin 2011, 89 ff. In trying to blame Burckhardt for his own tardiness, Overbeck lies about some details (see A. VERRECCHIA, *La catastrofe*, cit., 232) but his testimony as to Burckhardt's behavior is no less credible for that. [The biographer Janz holds that both Overbeck and Gast distorted Burckhardt's relationship to Nietzsche (C.P. JANZ, *Friedrich Nietzsche*, vol. 3, cit. 35–36), but there is no objective reason not to consider their eyewitness accounts as at least partially true. The best proof comes from the correspondence between Nietzsche and Burckhardt, where the latter always maintains an attitude of ironical distance (the Italian editor of the correspondence speaks of "deafening irony, sarcasm": M. GHELARDI, "L'argine e la marea: Jacob Burckhardt e Friedrich Nietzsche," in J. BURCKHARDT-F. NIETZSCHE, *Carteggio con un saggio di A. Warburg*, ed. M. Ghelardi, Aragno, Torino 2002, 61), without mentioning his attitude after Nietzsche's collapse, as, for example, his returning to sender the first volumes of Nietzsche's works.]

11. Kurt Liebmann in A. VERRECCHIA, *La catastrofe*, cit., 211.

12. [Recognition is due to Anacleto Verrecchia for bringing these testimonies to general attention, not however gratefully received by many Nietzschean admirers. The story behind these texts is quite singular and would deserve more than a footnote, as it gives an idea of the obstacles to be overcome in order to get a more realistic view of Nietzsche's life and personality. See note 14.]

13. E.F. PODACH, *Nietzsches Zusammenbruch*, Niels Kampmann Verlag, Heidelberg 1930, 112; A. VERRECCHIA, *La catastrofe*, cit., 271. [The visit happened January 14. Together with the quoted passage Verrecchia transcribes a treatment based on a cold shower and Sulfonal, while in Podach this detail is recorded January 15. I was not able to check the text in the original manuscript, though the detail is not so essential.] On the recurring image of the tyrant in Nietzsche's writings, see *Friedrich Nietzsche, Paul Rée, Lou von Salomé. Die Dokumente ihrer Begegnung*, Herausgegeben E. Pfeiffer, Insel Verlag, Frankfurt am Main 1970 (from now on NRS), 340 (NSB, vol. 6, 427), letter to F. Overbeck, August 14, 1883: "der 'Tyrann in mir.'" [On the clinical reports regarding Nietzsche see also C.P. JANZ, *Friedrich Nietzsche*, vol. 3, cit., 49 ff.]

14. [This is the most "tormented" document. Originally published in E.F. PODACH, *Nietzsches Zusammenbruch*, cit., but only partially and with no indication of the omissions, mostly regarding the more embarrassing passages. Following a well-grounded criticism, Podach soon published

the complete text in an article in a specialized medical journal: *Nietzsches Krankengeschichte* ("Die medizinische Welt," 4 [1930], 1452–1454). Janz declares that Podach's first publication was "flawless" and extols his prudence "for not disturbing Nietzsche's image (*das Bild Nietzsches trüben*)" given that such testimony "must not be left to the mercy of a technically senseless discussion" (*Friedrich Nietzsche*, vol. 3, cit., 54). It follows an attempt, evidently deemed technically appropriate, to explain Nietzsche's madness through his myopia. The result is that all scholars refer to Podach's first publication ignoring the complete text published in an obscure scientific journal normally not found outside medical libraries.]

15. E.F. PODACH, *Nietzsches Zusammenbruch*, cit., 119; E.F. PODACH, *Nietzsches Krankengeschichte*, cit., 1452; A. VERRECCHIA, *La catastrofe*, cit., 275.

16. [For the sake of clarity I will quote the German original of the cut passages, besides the most meaningful expressions as usual.]

17. The town where Nietzsche's family lived after his father's death.

18. A. VERRECCHIA, *La catastrofe*, cit., 275–278 [E.F. PODACH, *Nietzsches Zusammenbruch*, cit., 121–128 and complete transcription in E.F. PODACH, *Nietzsches Krankengeschichte*, cit., 1452–1453].

19. [The very power of what Girard calls metaphysical desire shows that it is by no means only destructive, but is, on the contrary, the destructive collapse of a force otherwise incredibly creative.]

20. NKS, vol. 13, *Nachlaß 1887–1889*, 14[166], 350.

21. NKS, vol. 13, *Nachlaß 1887–1889*, 16[1], 483.

22. See texts cited in A. VERRECCHIA, *La catastrofe*, cit., 76, with the symptomatic reference to Géraudel tablets [not Gérandel as wrongly transcribed in NKS, vol. 6, *Nietzsche contra Wagner*, 419, and vol. 15, 304 (mistake corrected in NB, III, 7/3, 1, 531); Auguste-Arthur Géraudel (1841–1906) was a famous French pharmaceutical manufacturer], also made in a letter of December 28, 1888 to Nietzsche's publisher Naumann to add the accent (NSB, vol. 8, 555) and in a draft letter of December 30 to Gast (NSB, vol. 8, 566; cf. A. VERRECCHIA, *La catastrofe*, cit., 174).

23. On the derisive, insulting treatment to which Nietzsche was subjected, see M. FINI, *Nietzsche*, cit., 358–359.

24. NSB, vol. 8, 578–579; A. VERRECCHIA, *La catastrofe*, cit., 181.

25. A. VERRECCHIA, *La catastrofe*, cit., 241; M. FINI, *Nietzsche*, cit., 345–346.

26. [Freud was not completely wrong in giving a great relevance to sex, which has much to do with our sense of body and identity. Starting from mimesis and mediation, there exists what I call an "objectual gravitation" towards some privileged objects of desire, and sex is no doubt one of the most important.]

27. This is the first version of a passage of *Ecce homo*, finally censored: "Frau Cosima Wagner has by far the most aristocratic nature that exists and, as regards myself, I have always interpreted her marriage to Wagner as adultery . . . the case of Tristan" (NKS, vol. 14, *Kommentar*, 473).

28. NKS, vol. 6, *Ecce homo*, 279.

29. Ibid., 281; Nietzsche repeats what he wrote in *Götzen-Dämmerung* (NKS, vol. 6, 64) with a slightly different sense.

30. [One of the few exceptions, influenced by Bataille and never mentioned by Girard, is P. KLOSSOWSKI, *Nietzsche et le cercle vicieux*, Mercure de France, Paris 1969, where the Nietzschean idea of eternal recurrence is linked to the traumas of his childhood, the following mental disease, and his triangular relationship with Richard and Cosima Wagner. Klossowski's inquiry provides an independent confirmation of my main assumptions, but in a highly speculative and partially misleading way, typical of the French Nietzscheanism of the period, strongly (and excessively) opposed by Girard.]

31. NKS, vol. 13, *Nachlaß 1887–1889*, 14[188], 374.

32. NKS, vol. 14, *Kommentar*, 762.

33. Fini argues surprisingly that since Nietzsche spoke no more about philosophy when he was insane, he was not insane when he philosophized (*Nietzsche*, cit., 375), failing to realize that the reasons for this were the same that, as insanity approached, brought an end to the violent migraines and fits of vomiting that had clearly been part of Nietzsche's medical history since youth, as Fini rightly says a few pages earlier (*Nietzsche*, cit., 367). Nietzsche ceased to speak about his philosophy because he had come to fulfill it in the flesh.

34. A. VERRECCHIA, *La catastrofe*, cit., 283.

Chapter 3. The Philosopher and His Double

1. [In my opinion this does not mean that in the contemporary world there is only rivalry, but that the old defenses against it, i.e., the collective mediations capable of transcending individual desires, are less and less effective.]

2. NKS, vol. 6, *Ecce homo*, 327; A. VERRECCHIA, *La catastrofe*, cit., 83–84. Nietzsche received *Parsifal* on January 3, 1878; the arrival of *Human, All Too Human* is recorded in Cosima's diaries on April 25, 1878 (*Die Tagebücher*, Band II 1878–1883, ed. M. Gregor-Dellin and D. Mack, Piper, München-Zürich 1977, 87; cf. C. WAGNER, *Diaries*, vol. II 1878–1883, Engl. transl. by G. Skelton, Harcourt Brace Jovanovich, New York-London 1980, 65: "At noon arrival of a new book by friend Nietzsche—feelings of apprehension after a short glance through it . . ."). This discrepancy is not simply inaccuracy on Nietzsche's part, as the more detailed account given in a letter to Lou Salomé on July 16, 1882 proves: NRS, 161–162 (here dated July 19/20, 1882; the correction is in NSB, vol. 7, 228–229).

3. Nietzsche was slightly wounded in the face in this absurd duel; cf. M. FINI, *Nietzsche*, cit., 44.

4. M. FINI, *Nietzsche*, cit., 26; the story of his fall downstairs, incredibly still supported by some scholars, was invented by Nietzsche's sister who was afraid that somebody might diagnose a hereditary defect in the family (cf. A. VERRECCHIA, *La catastrofe*, cit., 193).

5. NW, I, 2, 10[10], 260. [This is the third, and most poignant, draft of a writing of 1861 entitled *Mein Lebenslauf* and marked by an impressive crescendo: the first draft tries to demonstrate the existence of divine providence without saying anything more personal; the second presents briefly the shock of his father's death; the third repeats it with more dramatic details, ending with not completely convincing enthusiasm for the Pforta boarding school. But the event recurs in the many attempts to recount his own life that run throughout the juvenile writings of Nietzsche, and also plays a central role in a poem: NW I, 1, 4[77], 281–305; I, 2, 5[1], 3–4; 6[77], 122–123 (a poem centered on his father's grave: "meines Vaters Grab"); then we have the series of three drafts mentioned above: 10[8], 255–257; 10[9], 258–259; 10[10], 259–263; but the autobiographical vein does not stop here: I, 3, 15[41], 189–192; 15[42], 193–196; 18[2], 417–419; I, 5, 69[6], 40; 69[7], 40–41; 69[11], 45–50; 70[1], 52–54; 71[1], 55–57.]

6. This sense of guilt could well be at the root of his conviction that he had had a premonition.

7. NW I, 2, 13[12], 446–447; cf. C.P. JANZ, *Friedrich Nietzsche. Biographie*, vol. 1, Carl Hanser Verlag, München-Wien 1978, 110 ff. As we see, the only syphilis consciously present in Nietzsche (tabes is the final stage) was symbolic. [Nietzsche took inspiration from the character of Euphorion in Goethe's *Faust* Part II, the son of Faust and Helen doomed to die young, determining the failure of their marriage and the final destiny of the hero: this is a clearly symbolic choice reinterpreted by Nietzsche in a more infernal fashion, in which Friedrich becomes the Mephistophelian son of a Faust who has vanished.]

8. Letter to Raimund Granier, July 28, 1862 (NSB, vol. 1, 217). Cf. the singular ending to the letter to Franziska and Elisabeth Nietzsche on January 17, 1869, NSB, vol. 2, 362: "Ha ha ha! (Lacht) / Ha ha ha! (Lacht noch einmal.) / Schrumm! (Geht ab.) / F.N." ["Ha ha ha! (Laughs) / Ha ha ha! (Laughs again) / Scram! (Get out.) / F.N."] Undoubtedly, the ambivalent relationships to his mother and sister need to be analyzed to complete the picture of Nietzsche's mental state as a young man.

9. Letter of September 15, 1882 circa, in NRS, 230 (NSB, vol. 6, 258): "ein isolirtes Ungeheuer."

10. Letters to Emily Fynn, December 6, 1888 (NSB, vol. 8, 507: "Nietzsche, Unthier") and to Carl Fuchs, December 11, 1888 (NSB, vol. 8, 522: "das Unthier"; cf. M. FINI, *Nietzsche*, cit., 325, with the wrong date December 18).

11. [This remark was already pointing towards a conception of mimesis that differs from Girard, who takes no account of Friedrich's loss of his father.]

12. [Janz is right to speak of Wagner as an "Archetypus 'Vater'" (*Friedrich Nietzsche*, vol. 1, cit., 732).]

13. NKS, vol. 6, *Der Fall Wagner*, 52, footnote.

14. Letter of May 21, 1870 (NSB, vol. 3, 122).

15. Letter of June 24, 1872 (NSB, vol. 4, 15).

16. For details of Wagner's life, see for example R.W. GUTMAN, *Richard Wagner: The Man, His Mind, and His Music*, Harcourt Brace & Company, New York 1968 (Wagner's relations with Nietzsche are, however, distorted by Gutman's uncritical admiration for Nietzsche).

17. Entry for August 3, 1871, C. WAGNER, *Diaries*, vol. I 1869–1877, Engl. transl. by G. Skelton, Harcourt Brace Jovanovich, New York–London 1978, 399 (*Die Tagebücher*, Band I 1869–1877, Piper, München-Zürich 1976, 424); cf. A. VERRECCHIA, *La catastrofe*, cit., 83.

18. Entry for April 11, 1873 in C. WAGNER, *Diaries*, I, cit., 622 (*Die Tagebücher*, I, cit., 669).

19. NSB, vol. 4, 27.

20. NB, II, 4, 52–53; cf. C.P. JANZ, *Friedrich Nietzsche*, vol. 1, cit., 479; A. VERRECCHIA, *La catastrofe*, cit., 79.

21. Draft of October 29 (or just before), 1872, NSB, vol. 4, 76–77.

22. The word is transcribed correctly; without comment in the Italian and German editions, it is linked to cannibalism in the French edition. The etymology of "cannibalism" in German is the same as in Italian, making the wordplay fairly obvious: in other cases Nietzsche makes little *lapsus calami* in writing Latin words, showing himself to be a little less acquainted with this language than with Greek (see chapter 6, note 7).

23. [Cf. the use of Greek and Latin in Strindberg's answer to Nietzsche mentioned above.]

24. Letter of October 29, 1872 (NSB, vol. 4, 79).

25. NKS, vol. 6, *Ecce homo*, 286–287.

26. Ibid., 336.

27. A. VERRECCHIA, *La catastrofe*, cit., 34 (on relations with Lou Salomé) and elsewhere. Paul Rée, his friend and rival in regard to Lou Salomé, shows certain gay characteristics, and at times his friendship with Nietzsche takes on an ambivalent tinge, though this is always within a sphere of thoroughly repressed erotic implications (M. FINI, *Nietzsche*, cit., 136–139).

28. [This judgment may sound too severe, and no doubt Cosima's love for Wagner was sincere, but the first reasons for falling in love can appear deluding when looked at more closely. Anyway, it is enough to recognize some truth in my remarks to substantiate my argument. Much more could be said about Cosima's illegitimate origins and her desire to appear "hyper-German" as a reaction to her French education.]

29. C.P. JANZ, *Friedrich Nietzsche*, vol. 1, cit., 427.

30. [On the contrary the Wagners very much appreciated *The Birth of Tragedy*, which was sent to them a few days later: see entries for January 3–4 and 6, 1872 in C. WAGNER, *Die Tagebücher*, I, cit., 475–478; this could have been a clear sign of the path to be followed by Nietzsche to maintain a healthy and fruitful relationship with them.]

31. C.P. JANZ, *Friedrich Nietzsche*, vol. 1, cit., 496.

32. H. ALTHAUS, *Friedrich Nietzsche. Eine bürgerliche Tragödie*, Nymphenburger, München 1985, 278–279; cf. M. FINI, *Nietzsche*, cit., 114–115.

33. [Paranoia is of course a very bad lens for looking at reality: Nietzsche did not know that Cosima in her diaries defined the fourth *Untimely Meditation* as *"eine herrliche Schrift"* ("a splendid piece of writing"), and that King Ludwig in person had sent the Wagners a telegram thanking them "für die Nietzsche'sche Broschüre" ("for Nietzsche's pamphlet"): C. WAGNER, *Die Tagebücher*, I, cit., entries for July 1–11 and 21, 994–995. Anyway, the contrast with Wagner's triumph was crushing, as Janz himself finally recognizes in *Friedrich Nietzsche*, vol. 1, cit., 725–726.]

34. C.P. JANZ, *Friedrich Nietzsche*, vol. 1, cit., 356. As the evidence collected by Fini also makes clear, Nietzsche's psychosomatic reactions could be unbelievably intense. This suggests, among other things, that some of his ailments were a form of imitation of his father's illness.

35. C.P. JANZ, *Friedrich Nietzsche*, vol. 1, cit., 715.

36. Cf. M. FINI, *Nietzsche*, cit., 126 ff. (Fini makes the mistake of taking literally some of Nietzsche's venomous statements).

37. H.-L. Miéville in H. DE LUBAC, *Opera omnia*, ed. E. Guerriero, vol. 6, *Mistica e mistero cristiano. La fede cristiana*, Jaca Book, Milan 1979, 290.

38. [It is not a question of establishing a difference between "bad" or "good" mimesis, but of reaching a better understanding of its inner functioning as a unitary and plastic phenomenon. I now interpret its functioning in a more radical sense, as the possibility of exploiting mimesis creatively above all in its most intense manifestations, in themselves not destined to hostile and rivalrous collapse, but increasingly exposed to that danger.]

39. Fini sifts through the data scrupulously but he is without a mimetic view of desire and systematically misunderstands Nietzsche's senseless search after a model (e.g. *Nietzsche*, cit., 212 and 215). [Janz realizes Nietzsche's need for triangles, always without catching on to the triangular mediation, which on the contrary is one of the strong points of Girard's analyses:

see C.P. JANZ, *Friedrich Nietzsche*, vol. 1, cit., 628 ff. on the incredible proposal of marriage to Mathilde Trampedach *through* the model Hugo von Senger after having seen her only three times on normal social occasions; and ibid., vol. 2, Carl Hanser Verlag, München-Wien 1978, 280–281, on the ephemeral friendship with the young Resa von Schirnhofer, where the author notes the "verblüffender Parallel" (disconcerting parallel) to the relationship with Lou Salomé and Paul Rée, but without the presence of a third "go-between," and therefore without any forced and unlikely proposal of marriage like the one made to Lou.]

40. Letter to Hendrik Gillot in March 1882 in NRS, 102: "Ich kann weder Vorbildern nachleben, noch werde ich jemals ein Vorbild darstellen können. . . ."

41. [Made possible by the last period of universal mediations in the last European *ancien régime*.]

42. [This possibility does not seem to be seriously considered by the Girardian principle of "double mediation."]

43. [In the terms of my present theory of mediation, God's mediation was not sufficient to control human desires, as it requires the free collaboration of human beings.]

44. Gregory Bateson has studied the double bind in mother-child relationships and in the genesis of schizophrenia, while the Girardian theory utilizes the principle to describe the paradoxical structure of rivalry between imitator and model. [Subsequently I formulated the theory of the double bind as a creative matrix when it has been transcended, starting from Bateson's concept, but developing it in the human and cultural frame that he does not recognize specifically.]

45. [This would be completely impossible without the corresponding capacity of mediation *and* desire to create the very Being of human beings.]

46. [I am always stressing the creative potential of human mediations.]

47. NSB, vol. 4, 144–145.

48. Fini rightly defines the first *Untimely Meditation* as "a pure act of intellectual assassination" (*Nietzsche*, cit., 111). The mimetic transference was so intense that Nietzsche sarcastically attributed to Strauss the intention "to found the religion of the future," the precise role that he himself sought to incarnate a few years later (NKS, vol. 1, *Unzeitgemäße Betrachtungen*, 176).

49. Letter of March 2, 1873 (NSB, vol. 4, 131).

50. Letter of February 12, 1873 (NB, II, 4, 207; see also *Die Briefe Cosima Wagners an Friedrich Nietzsche*, ed. E. Thierbach, vol. II, Nietzsche-Archiv, Weimar 1940, 44).

51. Letter of February 19, 1883 (NSB, vol. 6, 333); cf. A. VERRECCHIA, *La catastrofe*, cit., 76. See also the letter to Malwida von Meysenbug, February 21, 1883: ". . . I think that this event, seen in perspective, is a cause of relief [*Erleichterung*] for me" (NSB, vol. 6, 335). This relief was anticipated by certain symptomatic images, masked in hypocrisy, in a letter to Wagner, dated May 20, 1874, written for the composer's birthday. Replying to Wagner who had noted that Nietzsche seemed to want to take steps to stay away, he says that he would like to measure time in lustra like the ancient Romans, who marked the completion of each five-year period with "great purificatory sacrifices [*grosse Reinigungsopfer*]" (NSB, vol. 4, 228). There can be no doubt: with the death of his adversary, the "great purificatory sacrifice" seems to have arrived.

52. A. VERRECCHIA, *La catastrofe*, cit., 76. It must be said that here, too, Nietzsche was not without models, if it is true that Wagner was overjoyed to learn that the detested Meyerbeer had died (M. FINI, *Nietzsche*, cit., 105).

53. Letter to R. von Seydlitz of February 24, 1887 (NSB, vol. 8, 32); cf. M. FINI, *Nietzsche*, cit., 293

[similar expressions recur in other letters of that period from Nice, to the point of writing to his mother (letter of March 2 or 3, 1887, NSB, vol. 8, 36) that in the entire French Riviera the earthquake caused "no more than 1000 deaths" (even though the sensitivity to the loss of human life was a little different from today)]. For Nietzsche's reactions, see also C.P. JANZ, *Friedrich Nietzsche*, vol. 2, cit., 514.

54. Letter from Overbeck to Gast, March 17, 1883 (NRS, 305). [Even more impressive is the subsequent testimony of Overbeck, who speaks in 1884 of an "alternation of states of deep depression and states of exaltation and euphoria generally characterizing persons doomed (*Kandidaten*) to madness. . . ." (*Erinnerungen*, cit., 68).]

55. The drafts can be dated to mid-February 1883 (NSB, vol. 6, 330–332). [Cosima destroyed all the letters received from Nietzsche.]

56. This article, *Il caso Wagner*, is included in G. D'ANNUNZIO, *Il caso Wagner*, ed. P. Sorge, Laterza, Rome-Bari 1996, 74 (cf. A. VERRECCHIA, *La catastrofe*, cit., 293). On October 25, 1888 Cosima got Richard Pohl to publish a reply to *The Case of Wagner* bearing the title *The Case of Nietzsche* (H. ALTHAUS, *Friedrich Nietzsche*, cit., 545) and in December Nietzsche had spoken to Gast and others about a plan to counterattack with the same title (NSB, vol. 8, letters to C.G. Neumann, to C. Fuchs, and to H. Köselitz of December 27, 1888, 553 and 555; cf. A. VERRECCHIA, *La catastrofe*, cit., 169). [In order to understand the polemical insistence on this title we should remember that *Fall* in German means both 'case' and 'fall.']

57. [In the first edition I used the term "refoundation to" inappropriately, since it is something new in comparison to the ancient foundations.]

58. G. D'ANNUNZIO, *L'innocente*, ed. M.R. Giacon, A. Mondadori, Milano 1996, 190.

59. Ibid., 191.

60. NKS, vol. 3, *Morgenröte*, IV, 296, 220.

61. G. D'ANNUNZIO, *L'innocente*, cit., 170.

62. R. GIRARD, *A Theater of Envy: William Shakespeare*, Oxford University Press, New York 1991, ch. 30, 271 ff.

63. [This hate rebounds on individuals, where they lack a super-individual mediation enabling them to find either a way to escape from rivalry or a proper way to ritualize it.]

64. NKS, vol. 6, *Ecce homo*, 357; the expression (coming after: "In this affair I have kept all the decisive pieces for myself—") appears all the more significant for substituting a more illusory: "I have time." Nietzsche really senses that he has no more time, and shows how intensely he depends on Wagner.

65. A. VERRECCHIA, *La catastrofe*, cit., 207.

66. [And without the absorbing force of superior mediation.]

67. [And, vice versa, mastering the doubles of art keeps one safe from the doubles of madness: their fertile use goes beyond the Girardian theorization.]

68. [Cf. the useful table in G. DELEUZE, *Nietzsche et la philosophie*, P.U.F., Paris 1973, 166.]

69. [We should not psychologize this attitude, whose cognitive repercussions will be dealt with in the next chapter.]

70. [Again, this undeniable circumstance remains unexplained if we fail to consider the creative

potential of mimetism even in unstable situations tending towards breakdown, such as Nietzsche's.]

71. Fini's assertion that Nietzsche "deep down [...] understands everything, absolutely everything about himself" (*Nietzsche*, cit., 264) is misleading: he has a *perception* of everything about himself, but refuses to understand it and accept it; had he done that, perhaps he would not have gone mad.

72. For the maladjusted Nietzsche's need to pretend, see M. FINI, *Nietzsche*, cit., 67–70.

73. NKS, vol. 5, *Jenseits von Gut und Böse*, II, 40, 57; Lou Salomé noted the importance of the mask and disguise in Nietzsche, in reference to this passage among others (L. ANDREAS-SALOMÉ, *Friedrich Nietzsche in seinen Werken*, Insel Verlag, Frankfurt am Main 1983, 40–41).

74. [Here we can observe the cognitive consequences of the most intense desire, which therefore does not coincide with Girard's internal mediation.]

75. Lacking the proper anthropological theory, unaware, in fact, that there is a fundamental anthropological problem, Jaspers defines Nietzsche's Dionysus as symbolizing "the *totality* of Being *in its unity*" [das *Ganze* des Seins *in eins*], which is true, but not in the speculative and abstract sense that he intends; and if "nobody has ever appropriated the symbol of Dionysus," it is precisely on account of this abstractness that avoids everything too vexatiously real (K. JASPERS, *Nietzsche. Einführung in das Verständnis seines Philosophierens*, De Gruyter, Berlin-New York 1981, 370–374).

76. [In my view such a study points towards a new type of philosophy, contrary to what Girard says.]

Chapter 4. The Foundation of Dionysus

1. [Referring to the desires of individuals left to themselves, in the growing isolation of contemporary society.]

2. [In the course of time I have come to give more and more importance to the divinization transference, which originally was a transfer of sacralization, since the proper representation of a single divinity was not possible, and I define it as the ecstatic source of culture. Today I consider the mimetic transference as a single ecstatic experience, that must be interpreted as the originary form of cultural mediation, much older than any form of desire, and that is detectable with differing degrees of success and transformation in all human mediations.]

3. H. DE LUBAC, *Mistica*, cit., 287.

4. For these topics, see G. FORNARI, "Labyrinthine Strategies of Sacrifice: *The Cretans* by Euripides," *Contagion: Journal of Violence, Mimesis, and Culture*, 1997 (4), 170, and, more fully, G. FORNARI, *Da Dioniso a Cristo*, cit., 72, 120–121.

5. [According to my interpretation the sacralization of violence theorized by Girard is only the beginning of a more complex and internal process that allowed the first cultural communities to use this new sacred center of their lives as a creative tool to know and define reality.]

6. NKS, vol. 1, *Homer's Wettkampf*, 784–785.

7. Ibid., 787.

8. Ibid., *Der griechische Staat*, 767.

9. Ibid., 768.

10. Ibid., 774.

11. NKS, vol. 13, *Nachlaß 1887–1889*, 16[16], 487.

12. T. MANN, *Politische Schriften und Reden*, vol. 1, *Betrachtungen eines Unpolitischen*, Fischer
    Bücherei, Frankfurt am Main-Hamburg 1968, 127 (see G. FORNARI, *Da Dioniso a Cristo*, cit.,
    11–12).

13. [My analysis here was influenced by Girard's powerful opposition of sacrifice to the Christian
    message; thus I did not consider the different layers recognizable (but not clearly distinguished)
    in D'Annunzio's and Mann's reflections, i.e., the necessity for political realism and even the
    possibility to use sacrifice as a Christian way of atonement; but the above argument still
    holds good if we keep in mind the danger of an extreme and one-sided development of those
    reflections.]

14. NKS, vol. 1, *Die dionysische Weltanschauung*, 571.

15. [Nietzsche became increasingly aware of the obstacle represented by Christianity and looked for a
    "third way" between sacrificial concealment and the Christian revelation of sacrifice.]

16. [It was precisely the unprecedented nature of this "new cult" that he sought to develop.]

17. Letter, April 14, 1887 (NSB, vol. 8, 57; cf. H. DE LUBAC, *Mistica*, cit., 296, with the wrong date
    April 16).

18. NKS, vol. 12, *Nachlaß 1885–1887*, 1[193], 54.

19. This question is dealt with in my article "Sacrificio, natura e differenza evangelica. Calasso e
    la visione sacrificale della natura da Anassimandro a Nietzsche," *Pluriverso*, 4 (2000), 28–44
    (German transl. "Dionysos, die Natur und die evangelische Differenz. Naturverstehen und Opfer:
    Calasso, Anaximander und Nietzsche," in *Das Opfer—Aktuelle Kontroversen*, ed. B. Dieckmann,
    Lit, Münster-Hamburg-London 2001, 37–58); cf. G. FORNARI, *Filosofia di passione*, cit.,
    205–226. [Nietzsche was at least partially conscious in doing this; cf. notes 42 and 44 in this
    chapter, and chapter 5, notes 42 and 47.]

20. NKS, vol. 13, *Nachlaß 1887–1889*, 15[110], 470.

21. NKS, vol. 12, *Nachlaß 1885–1887*, 1[162], 47.

22. Ibid., 1[163], 47: "...3. The wedding—and suddenly, while the heavens grow dark. / 4. Arianna."

23. See G. FORNARI, *Labyrinthine Strategies*, cit., 175; G. FORNARI, *Da Dioniso a Cristo*, cit., 80
    and 122.

24. G. D'ANNUNZIO, *Il Fuoco*, ed. N. Lorenzini, A. Mondadori, Milan 1996, 109–111.

25. Ibid., 171.

26. Ibid., 229.

27. [Perhaps we can also perceive a different national attitude here: more Catholic elasticity on the
    one hand, more Protestant seriousness on the other.]

28. T. MANN, *Der Tod in Venedig und andere Erzählungen*, Fischer, Frankfurt am Main-Hamburg
    1975, 62.

29. EURIPIDES, *Bacchae*, ed. E.R. Dodds, Oxford University Press, Oxford 1979, 8, line 139. See G.
    FORNARI, *Da Dioniso a Cristo*, cit., 120–121.

30. For an analysis of this episode in *The Magic Mountain*, see G. FORNARI, *Da Dioniso a Cristo*,
    cit., 5–13.

31. NSB, vol. 8, 578; cf. A. VERRECCHIA, *La catastrofe*, cit., 181.

32. NKS, vol. 6, *Ecce homo*, 348.

33. [Further confirmation of the cognitive relevance of Nietzsche's doubles.]

34. R. CALASSO, *Monologo*, cit., 161.

35. NKS, vol. 3, *Die fröhliche Wissenschaft*, III, 164, 498.

36. When his mother playfully scolded him for pilfering items in the asylum at Jena, he replied: "Now I shall have something to do when I crawl into my cave" (M. FINI, *Nietzsche*, cit., 353).

37. NKS, vol. 5, *Jenseits von Gut und Böse*, IX, 269, 223. [The same passage recurs in *Nietzsche versus Wagner*: NKS, vol. 6, *Nietzsche contra Wagner*, 434.]

38. L. ANDREAS-SALOMÉ, *Friedrich Nietzsche*, cit., 179–180; H. DE LUBAC, *Mistica*, cit., 294.

39. NKS, vol. 5, *Jenseits von Gut und Böse*, IX, 269, 224.

40. NKS, vol. 3, *Die fröhliche Wissenschaft*, V, 365, 613–614 (cf. NKS, vol. 6, *Götzen-Dämmerung*, 60–61).

41. NKS, vol. 2, *Menschliches, Allzumenschliches*, 348, 520.

42. [This amounts to seeking the 'third way' of sacrifice with 'eyes wide shut.']

43. NKS, vol. 3, *Morgenröte*, 45, 52.

44. [Here in part I was following Girard's argument about the ineffectiveness of sacrifice in the modern world, and for this reason I have distinguished now my present view from his without completely changing my old line of reasoning. Girard ignores the destructive/creative potential that can be released and exploited in this way, as Nietzsche himself dramatically shows.]

45. [Without the divinization that Nietzsche sought, a sign either of final despair or final hope.]

46. On nihilism, see the excellent summary in F. VOLPI, *Il nichilismo*, Laterza, Rome-Bari 1996, 45–52.

47. F. NIETZSCHE, *Frammenti Postumi 1888–1889*, cit., 23, 368–369.

48. [In order to avoid such nightmarish perspectives I would add that we must not rebuke Nietzsche moralistically in the name of superior values or theories, but understand what happened in his mind and in the European world.]

49. K. LÖWITH, *Nietzsches Philosophie der ewigen Wiederkehr des Gleichen*, Meiner, Hamburg 1986, 126 and 182.

50. [For a final evaluation of the Nietzschean idea of eternal recurrence see chapter 6 for the analysis of a very important testimony of Overbeck when he went to Turin.]

51. [In the sense that Löwith does not grasp the prophetic role of Nietzsche in this "tendency towards the extreme," a phrase that recalls the "montée aux extremes" of Girard's *Achever Clausewitz*. But we ought to consider the transformative resources possibly concealed in the human 'extreme.']

52. NKS, vol. 3, *Die fröhliche Wissenschaft*, III, 220, 509.

53. NKS, vol. 3, *Morgenröte*, IV, 252, 205.

54. Generally speaking, what has been written about Nietzsche and Christianity either embraces his theses uncritically or refuses to understand the precise cognitive reasons for his antagonism to the Christian message. Jaspers, for example, is perceptive in noticing a Christian influence at the

source of Nietzsche's criticisms, but cannot say what it consisted in precisely, or why the Christian content disappeared, i.e., Nietzsche lost his faith in God (K. JASPERS, *Nietzsche und das Christentum*, Piper, München 1963, 41 ff.). We are left as ever with the cliché of the death of God understood as his painless 'disappearance.'

55. [In the '90s, when I wrote these statements, I was following Girard's reflection on Christian revelation seeing it in strong terms of black and white. Now I am more inclined to think that revelation works in a way at one and the same time more complex and simpler: love may also prevail, even especially, in the midst of madness and violence.]

56. [That is, until he manages to be the ecstatic mediator of the whole community.]

57. NKS, vol. 13, *Nachlaß 1887–1889*, 15[110], 470.

58. [This is still apocalyptic in the Girardian manner, but we should not forget the motto *Bene navigavi, cum naufragium feci.*]

59. Letter of April 3/4 (NSB, vol. 6, 357). The differing reactions are interesting: friendly irony on the part of Malwida von Meysenbug, whose romantic idealism kept her far from realizing Nietzsche's intentions; unintentional irony from Elisabeth who was to base her future fortunes on the ideas of the new Antichrist: "I feel terrible [...] I really cannot see *who* might have the least use for them" (Letter to Franziska Nietzsche of April 4, in *Triangolo di lettere. Carteggio di Friedrich Nietzsche, Lou von Salomé e Paul Rée*, ed. M. Carpitella, Adelphi, Milan 1999, 283).

60. See R. GIRARD, *I See Satan Fall Like Lightning*, Engl. transl. by J.G. Williams, Orbis Books, New York 2001, 187–189; cf. G. FORNARI, *Da Dioniso a Cristo*, cit., 38–40.

61. [In my interpretation Christ's resurrection demystifies human violent foundations without rejecting our history and dependence on sacrifice, but using them as the only means of redemption.]

62. R. GIRARD, *Quand ces choses commenceront... Entretiens avec Michel Treguer*, Arléa, Paris 1994, 198.

63. Letter to Elisabeth, March 13, 1876 (NSB, vol. 5, 141) [though the reference to the goodness of a little lamb could be ironical].

64. [According to the Jewish and Christian myth Lucifer was an angel who rebelled against God; but it could be the contrary case of a self-proclaimed devil who becomes one and the same with the opposed God: light can be *contagious* in one way or another.]

Chapter 5. The Antichrist and the Crucifixion

1. M. MONTINARI, *Che cosa ha detto Nietzsche*, ed. G. Campioni, Adelphi, Milan 1999, 133 ff.

2. Ibid., 162–163.

3. [In their turn the so-called believers take Nietzsche's self-propaganda at its face value as a clear case of blasphemy but not to be taken seriously. We should not forget the conclusion of aphorism 125 in *The Gay Science*, when the madman is thrown out of the churches because he announces the death of God.]

4. A. VERRECCHIA, *La catastrofe*, cit., 103.

5. Ibid., 102.

6. "Nota introduttiva" to F. NIETZSCHE, *L'anticristo. Maledizione del cristianesimo*, Italian transl., Adelphi, Milan 1977, XI–XII.

7. G. COLLI, *Dopo Nietzsche*, Bompiani, Milan 1978, 168.

8. Nietzsche made ample use of L. TOLSTOY, *Ma Religion*, Paris 1885 (cf. NKS, vol. 14, *Kommentar*, 440–441; for the many fragments reporting or paraphrasing this work see NKS, vol. 13, *Nachlaß 1887–1889*, from 11[236] to 11[282], 93–109). As we know, Tolstoy denied the truth of the Resurrection and the Church's evangelical mission.

9. [These intuitions are evocative, and not reliable statements about the historical Jesus, who was part of the Jewish world and did not deny the sacred as such; incidentally a detail that Girard does not take into account.]

10. P. Burgelin in H. DE LUBAC, *Opera Omnia*, cit., vol. 2, *Il dramma dell'umanesimo ateo. L'uomo davanti a Dio*, Jaca Book, Milan 1992, 246, note 82 (De Lubac disagrees here, but strangely enough he omits to cite *The Antichrist* or related texts). [Even an accurate work like Janz's biography indulges in this fancy: *Friedrich Nietzsche*, vol. 1, cit., 823.]

11. NKS, vol. 13, *Nachlaß 1887–1889*, 14[38], 237 (see notes 13–15).

12. NKS, vol. 13, *Nachlaß 1887–1889*, 15[9], 409; see NKS, vol. 6, *Der Antichrist*, ch. 29, 200: "das Wort Idiot" (referring to Christ) and ch. 31, 202: "'kindliches' Idiothentum." [The idea of an insult addressed to the Crucified dates back to Nietzsche's juvenile writings: in the first line of the poem *Vor dem Crucifix* of April 1863 Christ on the cross is called a *blöder Narr*, a poor buffoon; see NW, I, 3, 15[1], 109.]

13. [And possibly indirect, through the articles, well known by Nietzsche, of the French critic E.-M. de Vogüé: see F. NIETZSCHE, *Epistolario 1885–1889*, ed. G. Campioni and M.C. Fornari, Adelphi, Milan 2011 (from now on NE), 1100–1101.]

14. On a Christological interpretation of Myskin see R. GIRARD, *Resurrection from the Underground: Feodor Dostoevsky*, ed. J.G. Williams, Crossroad, New York 1997, 78 ff. [Besides, De Vogüé interpreted Dostoevsky's character in a psychiatric way, and this perfectly fits with Nietzsche's use.]

15. And so there is no foundation for using Dostoevsky in an attempt to alleviate Nietzsche's insult. Still unhappier is the etymological explanation from the Greek *idiótes*, "a particular individual" (G. PENZO, *La filosofia dell'Anticristo*, preface to *L'Anticristo. Maledizione del cristianesimo*, ed. G. Penzo, Mursia, Milan 1982, 15), since Nietzsche's text actually speaks of idiocy in the physiological sense.

16. The most famous passage is *The Ass Festival* in Part IV of *Thus Spake Zarathustra* (NKS, vol. 4, *Also sprach Zarathustra*, 390–394); it is worth noting that a parody of the Crucifixion, in some graffiti discovered in Rome in 1857, depicts Christ with an ass's head. [A blatant merger of this insult with Nietzsche's antichristic proclamations occurs in *Ecce homo* (NKS, vol. 6, 302: "I am the *anti-ass* par excellence, and therefore a monster in world history—in Greek, and not only in Greek, I am the *Antichrist*."]

17. NKS, vol. 13, *Nachlaß 1887–1889*, 25[14], 644.

18. See references to Christ's schizophrenia in *The Antichrist* (again in ch. 31: NKS, vol. 6, 202) and to the *folie circulaire* (ch. 51: NKS, vol. 6, 231): the cyclothymia that Nietzsche ascribed to religious monomania.

19. NKS, vol. 10, *Nachlaß 1882–1884*, 1[70], 28.

20. NW, I, 5, 63[16], 15; the text is from 1868–1869 and because of its importance I quote it in German as well: "Was is fürchte, ist nicht die schreckliche Gestalt hinter meinem Stuhle sondern ihre Stimme: auch nicht die Worte, sondern der schauderhaft unartikulirte und unmenschliche Ton jener Gestalt. Ja wenn sie noch redete, wie Menschen reden!" Also referred to in H. ALTHAUS, *Friedrich Nietzsche*, cit., 239 ff., where there is an obvious effort to make light of it and play down its importance. [This awesome text shows us that Nietzsche was affected by a form of serious psychosis since his youth.]

21. Nietzsche's attitude of rivalry towards God has been noted before, but only in terms of a psychological reading or, at any rate, quite distinct from any wider anthropological frame (cf. H. DE LUBAC, *Il dramma*, cit., 243–244, and Y. LEDURE, "Il pensiero cristiano di fronte alla critica di Nietzsche," *Concilium. Rivista internazionale di teologia*, 5 [1981], 82–85). How the superman proceeds to become the antichrist is still, perhaps, best understood from Soloviev (V. SOLOVIEV, *I tre dialoghi e il racconto dell'anticristo*, Italian transl., Marietti, Genova-Milano 2002, 170–171).

22. R. GIRARD, *I See Satan*, cit., 180–181. [I do not agree with Girard's critical view of Nietzsche and Heidegger as fully part of the phenomenon described; see note 52 and chapter 6, note 33. Moreover, the persecution of the persecutors is something new, as it transforms persecution and makes it subtler.]

23. NKS, vol. 2, *Menschliches, Allzumenschliches*, I, 113, 116–117.

24. NKS, vol. 6, *Der Antichrist*, ch. 41, 214–215.

25. Expressions such as the 'justice,' 'honor,' or 'wrath' of God the Father indicate his transcendence in respect to the violent world of men. [The most profound aspect of these theological statements, going beyond the intentions of their authors, is that any realistic Christian reflection cannot dismiss sacrifice as a bad memory of the past, but must recognize it as a resource necessary for human beings, and must therefore transform sacrifice itself into a means of redemption.]

26. NKS, vol. 6, *Der Antichrist*, ch. 40, 214.

27. See in particular G. FORNARI, *Da Dioniso a Cristo*, cit., 343–345. [This is a meaningful difference between Girard's interpretation and mine: not unlike Nietzsche, and probably under the influence of structuralist textualism, Girard makes a comparison between the *stories* (= *mythoi*) of Dionysus and Christ, while I place special emphasis on the comparison between the events and their ritual reproduction (= sacrifice).]

28. [In the first version I wrote "model," which is partially true but too psychologistic: human beings need mediation first of all.]

29. [I have specified the Resurrection of Christ as an *experience* in order not to make it subjective but to stress its phenomenological (and, in my perspective, ecstatic) character: whatever we may think of the Resurrection, for the followers of Jesus it was their most powerful experience revealing the definitive meaning of his figure and message; therefore it was not a simple 'fact.']

30. [A clarification and strengthening of a non-persecutory use of human reason (not its invention) made possible by the recognition of that history and not its scandalized refusal.]

31. R. GIRARD, *La vittima e la folla. Violenza del mito e cristianesimo*, ed. G. Fornari, Santi Quaranta, Treviso 1998 [published only in Italian], 127–128; R. GIRARD, *I See Satan*, cit., 148 ff.

32. *II Thessalonians* 2, 3–7 [the epistle was probably written by a follower of St Paul, but this is not essential here]; the antichrist is theorized above all in *I John* 2, 18–23.

33. NKS, vol. 6, *Der Antichrist*, ch. 42, 215–216.

34. *Galatians* 5, 11 (cf. *I Cor.* 1, 23). In *I See Satan*, 45, Girard tends to partially underestimate the implications of this passage in Paul.

35. [I stress that this is Girard's interpretation not only to give him his due but also to make the reader aware that it is not simple to reconstruct Jesus' most likely way of reasoning: undoubtedly he was not speaking of any 'theory' of desire but of an objective force coming either from God or from Satan according to how we relate to it. In other words for him mediation (divine or diabolical) was different and more originary than desire.]

36. [The problem of the possible continuity of Christian tradition is real, of course, and we know today that there have been many different traditions inspired by Christ, starting from Jesus' message that was not strictly speaking 'Christian'; nevertheless, it is not a question of religious or ideological classification but of identifying an 'objective' ground to some extent common to all these branches and layers of the Christian tradition.]

37. [Substantial continuity is not absolute continuity, as is shown by the partially different meaning that Christ and his first followers (but it is true for most of Christian history) gave to *skandalon* and the related subjects of mediation, imitation, and desire.]

38. NKS, vol. 6, *Der Antichrist*, 219.

39. [While writing these remarks I was probably too dismissive in my turn, even though the tendency described is true. It is obvious that scientifically we have to study the Bible as a text not different from the others, but this does not mean that it has the same meaning.]

40. NKS, vol. 6, *Der Antichrist*, ch. 49, 228.

41. NKS, vol. 6, *Der Antichrist*, ch. 53, 235.

42. [In general, Nietzsche tends to hide violence and persecution when they could cast the blame on their authors, and to extol them when seen in their divinizing power.]

43. T. MANN, *Nietzsche's Philosophie*, cit., 36–38.

44. [This is the experiential and cognitive kernel of Christianity, and of Girard's thought as well, but it is in fact neither a 'theology' nor a 'theory'.]

45. Letter of September 1, 1886 in *Supplementa Nietzscheana*, vol. 1, F. OVERBECK, E. ROHDE, *Briefwechsel*, ed. A. Patzer, De Gruyter, Berlin-New York 1990, 109 (the letter contains a harsh critique of Nietzsche's whole work, mixing very acute statements with a lack of comprehension of its real core); cf. A. VERRECCHIA, *La catastrofe*, cit., 111.

46. NKS, vol. 6, *Der Antichrist*, ch. 53, 235. The final part, that begins with this phrase, is missing from the draft for ch. 53 (NKS, vol. 13, *Nachlaß 1887–1889*, 14[160], 345).

47. NKS, vol. 6, *Der Antichrist*, ch. 19, 185. [Further confirmation that Nietzsche was thinking about an unprecedented form of cult, not an impossible return to ancient sacrifice.]

48. NKS, *Der Antichrist*, ch. 53, 235.

49. [This is the climactic point of my analysis, and I believe it reveals a decisive step in Nietzsche's mental breakdown. While I was writing the text and now while commenting on it I experienced a real feeling of sorrow and pity for the author: my analysis remains to some extent ineffective if the reader does not share these feelings.]

50. NKS, vol. 6, *Ecce homo*, 312 quoting *Twilight of the Idols* (NKS, vol. 6, *Götzen-Dämmerung*, 160).

51. [In order to reach the final, definitive (= divine) clarity, of course.]

52. [I am not accusing Heidegger of a pro-Nazi attitude; for him it was mainly a momentary infatuation linked to real historical and cultural problems, not a serious ideological commitment. Just as D'Annunzio is not responsible for Fascism, so Heidegger is not responsible at all for Nazism, as shown by his being kept under special surveillance by the Gestapo after his resignation as rector of his university.]

53. NKS, vol. 6, *Der Antichrist*, ch. 56, 240.

Chapter 6. What None Have Perceived

1. H. MELVILLE, *Moby Dick*, cit., 366.

2. NKS, vol. 6, *Ecce homo*, 314.

3. I am following the version of F. NIETZSCHE, *Ecce homo*, ed. R. Calasso, cit., 125. In the version of the Colli-Montinari edition, the following conjectural reading is given: "30 September great victory; *Transvaluation* completed; a god takes his ease beside the river Po" (NKS, vol. 6, *Ecce homo*, 356); the hypothesis of a correction made by Nietzsche eliminated by an erroneous hypercorrection by Gast is ingenious but appears unnecessary (the basic meaning remains unchanged) and, in my opinion, banalizes the demented identification with God (it seems fairly unlikely that Nietzsche, now quite unbalanced, would let pass this umpteenth chance to declare his divine identity). In any case, the version preferred for this study was thought by Nietzsche, and it remains significant for my purposes.

4. NSB, vol. 8, 522.

5. A. VERRECCHIA, *La catastrofe*, cit., 195. [The destruction of this text is a much more unforgivable act than the many forgeries made by Elisabeth. For the German text see E. FÖRSTER-NIETZSCHE, *Das Leben Friedrich Nietzsche's*, Naumann, Leipzig 1895–1904, vol. II, 2, 921; cf. the comments of R. DI GIUSEPPE, *La catastrofe di Nietzsche*, in *Catastrofi generative. Mito, storia, letteratura*, ed. M. S. Barberi, Transeuropa, Ancona-Massa 2009, 100–101, that makes reference to my essay.]

6. [Riccardo Di Giuseppe holds that Nietzsche was alone responsible for his lynching as he was the one who abandoned all his friends (ibid., 108–109), but this reasoning is as acute as it is one-sided: the evidence shows that Nietzsche's strategy of self-destruction was perfectly compatible with real incomprehension and abandonment on the part of his friends and relatives, and makes his requests for help even more tragic.]

7. NKS, vol. 6, *Ecce homo*, 283.

8. NKS, vol. 13, *Nachlaß 1887–1889*, respectively 11[41], 21 (the passage reappears in the posthumous poetic fragments) and 16[50], 503.

9. Letter of January 10, 1869 (NSB, vol. 2, 357); the close is also symptomatic, with Nietzsche trying to exorcize the diabolical presences that came to infest his solitude: "*Absit diabolus! Adsit amicissumus* [*sic*, instead of *amicissimus*] *Erwinus!*" (Ibid.; "Out goes the devil! In comes most friendly Erwin!").

10. Rohde to Overbeck, January 24, 1889 (just after the catastrophe in Turin); F. OVERBECK, E. ROHDE, *Briefwechsel*, cit., 135.

11. Draft letter to Paul Rée and Lou Salomé written towards December 20, 1882 in NRS, 269 (NSB, vol. 6, 307).

12. To Rée, last week in December 1882 (NRS, 276; NSB, vol. 6, 309).

13. To Overbeck, December 25, 1882 (NRS, 279; NSB, vol. 6, 312).

14. In K. LÖWITH, *Nietzsche's Philosophie*, cit., 164.

15. Letter of August 26, 1883 (NRS, 344; NSB, vol. 6, 437; cf. H. DE LUBAC, *Mistica*, cit., 297).

16. NKS, vol. 12, *Nachlaß 1885–1887*, 5[79], 219.

17. Ibid., 1[1], 9.

18. NKS, vol. 6, *Ecce homo*, 276.

19. Ibid., 342.

20. Ibid., 302; NKS, vol. 4, *Also sprach Zarathustra*, 385. The poem reappears in the *Dionysian Dithyrambs* with significant changes (NKS, vol. 6, *Dionysos-Dithyramben*, 382–387). Luther's words are first quoted in a letter to Paul Rée towards the end of July 1878, reversing the phrases in an attempt to be reassuring: "So help them *God—I* cannot do otherwise" (NRS, 50; NSB, vol. 5, 342).

21. Letter of December 16, 1888 (NSB, vol. 8, 528); cf. A. VERRECCHIA, *La catastrofe*, cit., 155.

22. NKS, vol. 6, *Dionysos-Dithyramben*, 390–392.

23. The collective presence of these vultures, looming over Nietzsche in his solitude, is already apparent in his writings in 1872–1873 (see C.P. JANZ, *Friedrich Nietzsche*, vol. 1, cit., 505).

24. [At the same time, to attenuate the severity of this quotation, it should be said that the body remains the Christian premiss for resurrection.]

25. NKS, vol. 6, *Nachlaß 1887–1889*, 21[2]; 21[3], 579–580.

26. H. DE LUBAC, *Il dramma*, cit., 103–105.

27. [In the first version I wrote: "definitive victory." This was excessive, the victory of the Cross is in the world but is not of this world. For this reason now I write: "silent victory."]

28. A. VERRECCHIA, *La catastrofe*, cit., 128.

29. T. MANN, *Nietzsche's Philosophie*, cit., 25.

30. On the cross see G. FORNARI, *Da Dioniso a Cristo*, cit., 289–356.

31. Ibid., 24–25.

32. [In a new technical and industrialized fashion, as shown by Hannah Arendt's analyses of totalitarianism.]

33. T. MANN, *Nietzsche's Philosophie*, cit., 40.

34. [In the first version I followed Girard in recalling Nietzsche's responsibility in paving the way for Nazi ideology, but today I do not think it is a proper evaluation: Hitler and the other leading Nazis simply interpreted in the worst possible sense what Nietzsche had detected in advance and in complete isolation. Such an attribution of responsibility was not really part of my argument and unwittingly amounts to scapegoating poor Nietzsche.]

35. NKS, vol. 6, *Ecce homo*, 374.

36. NSB, vol. 8, 573; cf. A. VERRECCHIA, *La catastrofe*, cit., 178–179.

37. [The message, made known by S. BARBERA, *Un biglietto smarrito di Friedrich Nietzsche a Jean*

Bourdeau, gennaio 1889, "Belfagor," LIV (January 1999), 74–78, is undoubtedly authentic. It is quoted in French by Bourdeau, who received two final notes from Nietzsche, and, in a book published in 1904, he describes the content of the second in these terms: "Le lendemain, seconde lettre, où il nous confiait qu'il était le Christ en personne, le Christ crucifié" ["The day after, a second letter, where he confided to us that he was the Christ in person, Christ crucified"] (NB III, 7/3, 2, 835); the message is quoted more completely in a letter of December 31, 1889 from the French Germanist Henry Lichtenberger to Elisabeth: "... la second [lettre] était en italien et ne contenait que qq. mots: 'Je suis le Christ, le Christ lui-même, le Christ crucifié'" ["... the second letter was in Italian and contained only a few words: etc."] (NB III, 7/3, 1, 553). The date of the second letter must be January 2, 1889. This message is extraordinary and should be inserted in the main text of the critical edition, and not in a simple footnote where non-specialist readers or scholars can easily miss its presence or significance (it would be like excluding from the authentic texts of a pre-Socratic a fragment surviving in a Latin translation but not in Greek). Collating the two versions we might even obtain a likely retroversion in Italian, especially since Bourdeau tells Lichtenberg that he remembers the message by heart (*par coeur*): "Io sono il Cristo, il Cristo in persona, il Cristo crocefisso" (Italian text in NE, 1322–1323). I would add that Bourdeau's testimony is less complete but more faithful to the typical Italian expression 'in persona' (if the expression were 'il Cristo stesso' a Frenchman would probably translate 'le Christ même'), while Lichtenberg's testimony restores the complete text. The article is of course Christological. The only uncertainty is over the orthography of "crocefisso"; "crocifisso" is also possible, with the slight advantage of an orthographic analogy with the Latin *crucifixus*.]

38. [In this sense we might interpret the frequent use of Italian at the Jena clinic, even though in an unhinged and less than elementary way as recorded in the *Krankenjournal* (E.F. PODACH, *Nietzsches Zusammenbruch*, cit., 120; E.F. PODACH, *Nietzsches Krankengeschichte*, cit., 1452–1453).]

39. [C.P. JANZ, *Friedrich Nietzsche*, vol. 3, cit., 32–33.]

40. [Ibid., 39.]

41. [Ibid.]

42. [As hypothesized by C.P. JANZ, *Friedrich Nietzsche*, vol. 3, cit., 34, because of Nietzsche's nearsightedness (although Janz gives little credit to this local tradition).]

43. For the eyewitness accounts, see A. VERRECCHIA, *La catastrofe*, cit., 211–216 [the very contradictions of the accounts support their real origin. It is not therefore correct that the scene has never been documented, as stated in NE, 1229].

44. [An analogy already noted in L. MITTNER, *Storia della letteratura tedesca*, vol. 3, t. I, Einaudi, Torino 1971, 821.]

45. A. VERRECCHIA, *La catastrofe*, cit., 54–55: letter to Reinhart von Seydlitz of May 13, 1888 (NSB, vol. 8, 314); NKS, vol. 13, *Nachlaß 1887–1889*, 14[166], 350. The hypothesis is that the already mentioned fragment of a man who beats his horse and then urinates on it might be the transformation of Dostoevsky's scene, through Nietzsche's 'scatological' will to power. According to Janz (*Friedrich Nietzsche*, vol. 3, cit., 35), there is no proof of a link to Dostoevsky. However, the analogies between the episode in *Crime and Punishment* and eyewitness accounts in Turin (where Dostoevsky's novels were certainly not widely known at the time), with the intermediary factor of comparable passages in Nietzsche's own works, support the truth of the episode and suggests the influence (possibly indirect) of the literary scene on Nietzsche.

46. A. VERRECCHIA, *La catastrofe*, cit., 212.

47. *Matthew* 12, 31–32.

48. *Hebrews* 10, 31, referring to those who scorn "the Spirit of grace" (10, 29).

49. H. DE LUBAC, *Mistica*, cit., 298.

50. Letter of December 30, 1888 (NSB, vol. 8, 566).

51. NKS, vol. 6, *Dionysos-Dithyramben*, 404–405.

52. NW I, 3, 17[14], 391: "Dem unbekannten Gotte."

53. NKS, vol. 4, *Also sprach Zarathustra*, 313–317.

54. NKS, vol. 6, *Dionysos-Dithyramben*, 401.

55. [Here again I originally wrote "triumphantly," but the triumph of the Lamb appertains to a different level of reality.]

Index